Transactional Skills

Transactional Skills

Contract Preparation and Negotiating (What to Do—and What Not to Do)

SECOND EDITION

Peter Siviglia

CAROLINA ACADEMIC PRESS
Durham, North Carolina

Library of Congress Cataloging-in-Publication Data

Names: Siviglia, Peter, author.
Title: Transactional skills : contract preparation and negotiating (what to do - and what not to do) / by Peter Siviglia.
Description: Second edition. | Durham, North Carolina : Carolina Academic Press, 2025. | Includes bibliographical references and index.
Identifiers: LCCN 2024054921 | ISBN 9781531032920 (paperback) | ISBN 9781531032937 (ebook)
Subjects: LCSH: Contracts--United States. | Legal composition. | Contracts.
Classification: LCC KF807 .S583 2025 | DDC 346.7302/2--dc23
LC record available at https://lccn.loc.gov/2024054921

CAROLINA ACADEMIC PRESS
700 Kent Street
Durham, North Carolina 27701
(919) 489-7486
www.cap-press.com

Printed in the United States of America

for Anne

ANNIVERSARY

I would take from Them a line
to define a thought—
that time is but invention,
an artifact of mind
to mark the flow and cycle of events:
harbors carved in space to brace a passage,
give it place.

But this is mere convenience … at best,
for science a necessidence.
As to the rest: all occurs
and will occur as if by fate,
without need-reference to a date.

The tiger knows no days.
He marks not births nor kills
with celebrations at appointed times,
but moves in a continuum of grace,
an elegance
amid a forest of the mind.

I will not then pretend to mark a date for you
to celebrate the counterfeit of some event.
Instead I will spend all these days with you
in equal celebration of all that you have meant.

Contents

Part II
Contract Basics; Basic Terms; Basic Agreements

About the Book

Transactional Skills has three parts. Together, these three Parts provide comprehensive, realistic instruction that lays a sound foundation for any lawyer practicing in the realm of commercial transactions.

Part I introduces the writer to the rules and discipline required to prepare a proper and an effective contract. These rules include ethical considerations. Part II treats (i) basic and important contract terms, (ii) building agreements, especially in large, complex transactions, and (iii) some of the most basic and common agreements. Part III reveals the essentials to negotiate deals properly, effectively and ethically.

Part II also contains, wherever appropriate, references to drafting problems contained in *Exercises in Commercial Transactions*, Carolina Academic Press, revised edition 2019. Suggested solutions and commentary accompany each problem. If desired, each problem with the accompanying solution and commentary can serve as a case study.

In addition, wherever appropriate, under the heading "Resource Materials" that appears at the end of a chapter, and elsewhere in the text, Part II contains references to model contracts in *Commercial Agreements—A Lawyer's Guide to Drafting and Negotiating*, Thomson Reuters, supplemented annually. These materials illustrate the principles discussed in Part II. Westlaw makes them available to law students and their teachers without charge if the law school has a Plan with Westlaw that includes *Commercial Agreements*.

Some prerequisites for a course using *Transactional Skills* are contracts, corporations and other business entities, and, if possible, a course in the Uniform Commercial Code.

Although a few of the Recourse Materials have not yet been published, Peter is a bit of a compulsive nerd, and has already written and edited the unpublished materials. He will be happy to provide any of those materials to teachers on request. Requests should be sent to him at psiviglia@aol.com.

Peter also adheres to Dirty Harry's maxim in *Magnum Force*: "A man has got to know his limitations." So he welcomes comments and suggestions.

Acknowledgments

Anne K. Siviglia, teacher of writing at the Hackley School, Tarrytown, NY (author's personal editor).

Keith Sipe, Publisher, Carolina Academic Press, for suggesting this book.

Kay Sugahara (1909–1988); **Peter J. de Savary**; **Michael Sarch**. Their deals made this book possible!

TJ Smithers; **Rachael Meier**; **Arthur Iannacone**, Carolina Academic Press, whose diligence and dedication to their jobs improved the quality of this work.

About the Author

Peter Siviglia was born in Brooklyn, New York, about the time the Dead sea was just beginning to feel ill. He is now semi-retired from the practice of law, spending much of his time writing about contract preparation and teaching his grandchildren the games he played on the streets of Brooklyn.

Peter received a BA from Williams College in 1961, an MA from Brown University in 1962, and a JD from Harvard University in 1965.

Peter has practiced law in New York for more than 50 years, mostly in Manhattan, representing clients both domestic and foreign, public and private. He has served as correspondent counsel and as special counsel to major international law firms on contract matters and negotiating.

In addition to Transactional Skills, he is the author of one of West Group's best-selling works in the commercial field: *Commercial Agreements—A Lawyer's Guide to Drafting and Negotiating*, Thomson Reuters, supplemented annually. He is also the author of three works published by Carolina Academic Press: *Writing Contracts, a Distinct Discipline*; *Exercises in Commercial Transactions*; and *Contracts and Negotiating for the Business Person*; and a book of poetry and other writings, *The Sidelines of Time*, Archway Publishing.

In addition, Peter has written numerous articles on writing contracts and other legal topics. He also lectures on contract preparation and business transactions for CLE programs.

All of Peter's contracts that have been involved in litigation—and there have been very few—have been enforced against the defaulting party, without exception on summary judgement, based solely on the words of the contract. In one case a Federal District Court in New York, quoting the entire agreement in its opinion, wrote "Nothing could be more clear..."; and a Texas appellate court, in a unanimous three-judge opinion, repeatedly citing the contract's "clear wording" and "unambiguous" text, concluded that "Under the Agreement's unambiguous language ... [the defendant] must pay the Fee" ($21 million).

Part I

Writing Contracts: A Distinct Discipline

Chapter 1

Les Preludes

A few thoughts before we begin:

1. Your writing is your mind walking naked across the page.

1A. Essential Corollary: The discipline of writing well improves the quality of your thinking.

2. The two certainties in life: Death and Taxes. Well it's time to add a third: Mistakes.

   Only Mozart, according to legend, got it right on the first try.

3. What the wheel is to the world of mechanics, grammar is to the world of writing. As the author, Stephen King, said: "Bad grammar produces bad sentences." And bad sentences are the fabric from which litigators style their suits.

4. The task of transactional attorneys is to place commercial litigators on the endangered species list.

And that last *Prelude* is what the remainder of this book is about.

Chapter 2

The Transactional Attorney

Law schools, for the most part, have been training students to be litigators. Students learn to examine the facts of a case and the applicable law in order (1) to develop arguments to support a position in a contentious situation, and (2) to determine the likely outcome of a controversy. This training prepares the student to represent a client in a purely adversarial situation.

The role of the commercial lawyer is different. True, there is an adversarial aspect to every commercial transaction. But every commercial transaction always involves two or more parties trying to reach a common goal, that is, a deal, such as a partnership to conduct a business, or an employment arrangement, or a loan, or the sale of a business. As these examples illustrate, the level of commonality will vary with the transaction: high in the first two; less in the latter two. Nevertheless, in all transactions, the parties must reach a working relationship. And to achieve this result, cooperation and even compromise are required, for what is gained by success should, at least logically, be worth more than what is surrendered to achieve it. Thus, an appreciation and respect for what is important to each participant and an effort by all to honor the concerns of the others are essential. Sometimes—not often—the concerns are too disparate to be reconciled, and the deal will fail; but no deal should fail for lack of imagination and enterprise diligently directed to coordinate the interests of all. And the lawyer, while representing the interests of his or her client, must play an important role in this process.

The thought process of the commercial lawyer, therefore, differs from that of the litigator. The commercial lawyer is an architect and engineer of relationships, and the homes which these attorneys design are the agreements or private legal arrangements within which their clients operate. Thus, the commercial attorney must think <u>first</u> in terms of the various considerations involved in each transaction (for example, a non-compete covenant in an employment agreement), then in terms of how to treat each of these considerations (scope of the activities restricted, period, and geographical extent of the covenant), and finally (and here the attorney takes on the aspect of a builder) in terms of writing the words to embody the decision or the result of the negotiation; for if that decision is not transcribed correctly, the consequences can be the same as those that arise from a defect in construction.

The final function of the commercial attorney, that of the writer, is the most solitary of the three. The first two—determining the considerations and determining how to deal with them—are performed in conjunction with the client and the attorneys for the other parties. The attorney performs the last—and mechanically the most difficult—alone: either preparing the initial draft or examining the draft of another. And here, too, the skill of the commercial lawyer differs from that of the litigator. The litigator's writing is expository. The litigator is writing a thesis. The litigator is writing to convince. The commercial attorney, on the other hand, is writing a set of rules and instructions, the specifications for a business relationship or a transaction: the law of the deal. It is precision writing, and the draftsperson must always be aware that it is easier for a lawyer to pass through the eye of a needle than to write a sentence that means the same to the writer as well as to everyone else who reads it. Thus, in the editing process, following the initial draft, the writer must assume the role of an objective, adversarial critic.

The primary purpose of this book, though, is not to teach the student how to write a particular type of agreement or how to deal with a particular issue, for each agreement and each issue, like each case with which the litigator deals, must be treated in terms of its own unique circumstance. The primary purpose of this book is to develop a way of thinking and a set of skills and techniques that will allow the student to deal effectively with those situations that the student will encounter as a practicing attorney.

Chapter 3

What Is a Contract?

As stated in Chapter 2, a contract is simply a set of instructions, *i.e.*, the specifications for a transaction or a business relationship or both. It is a unique form of writing. Unlike expository writing, it does not seek to inform as does this book, and it does not seek to persuade like a brief. Unlike creative writing, it does not seek to entertain like a novel or a poem or a play. In fact, my wife, who teaches English, is now convinced that the contract is a unique, third form of writing, requiring a discipline different from the disciplines required for expository or creative writing.

Being a set of instructions, the contract demands precision writing, for the consequences of drafting errors are measured in dollars. One of the favorite watering holes of commercial litigators is the Ambiguity Bar, and they forage in the forest of Poor Editing.

By way of contrast, flaws in creative or expository writing are usually of little significance. For example, I understand that a reader once asked the poet, Robert Browning, what a line in one of his poems meant. Browning looked at the poem, focused on the line, and then replied: "When I wrote that line God and I knew what it meant. Now only God knows."

Scholars have isolated flaws in *The Great Gatsby*. And there are other flaws that the scholars have not recognized. Yet, despite these flaws, *The Great Gatsby* remains a great novel, frequently studied, and creating enjoyment, and causing no harm.

Obviously, creative writers and their works, sprinkled with imprecision and ambiguity, thrive. Likewise flaws in expository writing can be explained and corrected without harm to anyone. But flaws in plans and specifications or in their execution can be disastrous: They can result in the collapse of a bridge such as the collapse in 2018 of the pedestrian bridge in the Miami area. In a contract they too can result in disaster, though not necessarily fatal: dispute and litigation, where the only sure winners are the lawyers.

No easy task is it to write with precision, for one of the most difficult endeavors is to write a sentence that can have but one meaning to all who read it: that meaning being the one intended by the draftsperson. That everyone "knows what was intended" is not good enough. With time, recollection fades and alters; and, more to the point, when the dispute arises, the litigators for each side will scrutinize every aspect of the document for an advantage, for a loophole, or for a place to hide.

In my youth, back in the Jurassic period, I remember reading about a case that hinged on a prepositional phrase. An employee quit her employment and moved, claiming severance payments. The company contested her claim, asserting that she was not entitled to the payments because she left voluntarily. The employee's contract provided that she was entitled to the payments "on termination of her employment by the Company". The employee read "by the Company" as modifying "employment"; the company, on the other hand, argued that the phrase modified "termination"—that is, she was only entitled to severance *on termination by the company* of her employment. Although, grammatically, the employee had the better argument (generally, an adjectival, prepositional phrase modifies the noun to which it is closer), the issue is not free from doubt.

From the employee's point of view, the text should have read "on termination of her employment with the Company"; from the company's perspective, it should have read "on termination by the Company of her employment". Nitpicking? Perhaps, but someone's money flowed on the turn of the nit.

Yes, treatises can be written—and they have been written—on the many rules and fine points of grammar. But I am old, and this is not the place for such a treatise. Besides, a lawyer drafting a contract does not have time to consult a reference work on every phrase. If the lawyer went into that level of detail, the contract would never be written. In fact, only in special circumstances will an attorney even check the law on a point the attorney is drafting. What the lawyer must do, therefore, is examine the document as if someone whom the lawyer hates had written it, and as if the finest litigator on the planet were going to review it from an adversarial point of view. The lawyer must become sensitive, not to legalese, but to the English language, to what the words are actually saying rather than what the lawyer intends or expects them to say.

As illustrated by the example of the employment agreement cited above, the difficulty, the greatest danger to the writer, and the writer's greatest weakness, are that the writer is inclined to read his or her own words to mean what the writer intends them to mean—not what they actually say.

And on that cautionary note, let's move to our next chapter.

Chapter 4

The Prime Directive; Implementing the Prime Directive

4.1 The Prime Directive

A contract being a set of instructions, the prime directive must be: *State the direction accurately and as simply as possible.* I purposely did not say: "State the direction clearly", because a direction can be clear:

- "Excuse me, can you tell me where the ladies' room is?"
- "The ladies' room? Yes. Straight down this hall, first door on your right."

Clear? Yes, but wrong: The first door on the right is the men's room. Accuracy and simplicity are, therefore, the goals; in combination, they produce clarity.

The prime directive purposely reads: "State the direction accurately and <u>as simply as possible</u>"—not "accurately and simply". Sometimes the concepts, themselves, are complex, so the transcription cannot always be "simple" in the purest sense. In writing contracts, "simple" is relative; of necessity, it is a function of accuracy, which is paramount. This dependency, though, must not become an excuse for laziness. The lawyer must fight—that is, the lawyer must edit and re-edit—to state even complex terms as simply as possible.

If you are having trouble sleeping, see the phantom stock plan in Chapter 6A of *Commercial Agreements*, *supra*. Valuation of the stock is an essential part of the plan, and the valuation formula is an example of why "simple" in the purest sense cannot always be achieved. The lawyer did not concoct the formula. The lawyer's function was to transcribe that formula correctly and as simply as possible, so that when applied step by step, it would produce the intended result.

4.2 Techniques and Rules to Implement the Prime Directive

A. Read the text aloud—especially complicated provisions.

Reading the provisions aloud will often reveal an error that may hide successfully when the text is read silently. Compared to reading silently, reading aloud requires the reader to focus on each word and, therefore, to read more slowly. This more deliberate process allows the mind a better chance to grasp the literal meaning of the words and hopefully to compare that meaning with the message actually intended.

In over fifty years of practice, "time of the essence" has never been a factor or consideration in any transaction.

Having another attorney read the contract can also be helpful, but this assistance is not a substitute for the draftsperson's responsibility. The draftsperson should understand the transaction as well as if not better than anyone else, and so the draftsperson generally should be the best qualified to determine whether the language correctly transcribes the parties' intent.

B. Be patient—set document aside; revisit.

Setting the contract aside for a while—preferably overnight—and then rereading it is also a useful device and probably the most effective editing tool. The period of separation from what the writer has written creates an objectivity that reading the words over and over without a break fails to accomplish. By setting the contract aside, the writer, on returning to the text, will more likely read the text as if someone else had written it—that is, more critically.

Also, when experiencing difficulty in conceiving or writing a particular provision, it is often helpful to work on another part of the agreement or to stop altogether and turn to something else, rather than trying to force a solution. This separation will allow the mind to work on the problem subconsciously, without pressure, as it does when a person cannot remember a name or a place and, after moving to another subject, recalls the information sometime later.

C. State the instruction once; avoid repetition.

If repetition is necessary, use the same language in each instance in order to avoid the risk of different interpretations, which are fabrics from which litigators style their suits.

D. Be careful in placing modifiers, especially modifying phrases and clauses.

The example of the severance-pay dispute in Chapter 3 attests to one of the most common problems in drafting: placement of the modifier. The writer knows his or her intent and automatically associates the modifier with the term it should modify. The reader, however, does not reside between the writer's ears, so to the reader the meaning can be quite different—even humorous (or perhaps insulting):

> Dear Bill,
>
> As you do not wish to exercise your options at this time, I am returning your check and the notice of exercise. I just don't feel real comfortable sitting on a check from anyone of this size.

Here are two more examples of poor placement of a modifier and the corrective surgery, which, hopefully, you will find helpful:

- Note the literal difference in meaning between the following two sentences, though the writer's intent in the first is clearly the statement made in the second. I detected the flaw after setting the document aside for a while and then reading it out loud.

  Never include a provision in a contract which you do not understand.

  vs.

  Never include in a contract a provision which you do not understand.

  Place the clause next to the word it modifies.

  Better yet, rewrite the sentence eliminating the clause

  Never include a provision in a contract if you don't understand the provision.

- Ambiguous: "The fee will not be payable with respect to renewals or extensions of contracts which are concluded after the year 2000." (Two possible antecedents for the word "which")

  Intended: "The fee will not be payable with respect to a renewal or extension of any contract if the renewal or extension is concluded after the year 2000."

Rewrite the sentence eliminating the clause

Errors in placement are most readily recognized by setting the document aside for a while and then rereading it.

D.1 Beware: Ambiguous Use of Pronouns.

For example:

John wrote to Bob every day while he was away.

To whom does "he" refer, John or Bob?

Corrected: John wrote to Bob every day while John was away.

Repeat the noun. Avoid the pronoun.

* * *

As you have seen from the foregoing examples, ambiguity is a mighty enemy. Ambiguity is a playground for litigators!

Help attune your mind to ambiguity through your expository writing: letters, emails, and memoranda. Take the same care in your expository writing as you would writing a contract.

E. Punctuate carefully.

Careless punctuation can result in an unwanted meaning:

Let's eat Grandma vs. Let's eat, Grandma

And careless punctuation can result in litigation. Truck drivers of the Oakland Dairy company in Maine argued that they were entitled to overtime pay because the following statutory exclusion from the overtime pay did not apply to them as "distributors":

(ii) Overtime rules do not apply to:

The canning, processing, preserving, freezing, drying, marketing, storing, packing for shipment or distribution of:

(1) Agricultural produce;
(2) Meat and fish products;
(3) perishable food.

The court was asked whether the exclusion applied to time spent on "packing for ... distribution" or whether it applied separately to the actual "distribution" by the truckers of the three items mentioned. The issue hinged on the lack of a comma following the word "shipment":

packing for shipment or [for] distribution of

vs.

packing for shipment, or distribution of

The Court held for the truckers: $5 million in overtime pay for the truckers.

Another stunning example of litigation over a comma appears in item "M" below. It does pay to know grammar!

F. Choose the right words and the right grammatical structure.

A common provision in contracts is that notice be given by a certain time. Often the clause will read "within thirty days of _X_ date". This expression can apply either to the thirty days before or to the thirty days after _X_ date. Depending on the intent, the provision should read "within thirty days [*prior to* _X_ date // *following* _X_ date // *before or after* _X_ date]".

Lawyers are fond of using the words "such" and "said" to avoid repeating long expressions, but if there are two possible antecedents, an ambiguity can result:

> ... will pay $10,000 on each anniversary of the delivery and acceptance of the ship under this charter commencing with the second anniversary of such delivery and acceptance provided none of the following events of default has occurred prior to such anniversary: ...

vs.

> ... will pay $10,000 on each anniversary of the delivery and acceptance of the ship under this charter commencing with the second anniversary of such delivery and acceptance provided none of the following events of default has occurred prior to the date on which the payment is due: ...

Two other words that frequent agreements are "herein" and "hereof": for example, "as provided herein" or "in accordance with the terms hereof". In each of these expressions, the word "herein" or "hereof" can refer to the entire agreement or to the section of the agreement in which the word appears. Unless the meaning is unambiguously clear from the context, the client is better served by using a few extra words: "as provided in this agreement" or "as provided in this section".

G. Never use terms of art.

Terms used to abbreviate broad concepts: "right of first refusal", "after tax earnings", per share earnings on a "fully diluted" basis, should never be used because these terms comprehend too many variables.

The term "right of first refusal" by itself is an invitation to a lawsuit. Chapter 20, "Options", reveals the reasons.

Often valuations are based on "after tax earnings" during a specific period, but like "right of first refusal", the term by itself is incomplete. Should tax items that arise outside the relevant period (*e.g.*, loss carry-forwards) be included in or excluded from the determination? Should extraordinary items of income or loss be included or excluded? Should earnings be calculated on a consolidated or unconsolidated basis?

When per share earnings are on a "fully diluted" basis, shares that can be acquired under options or other rights usually comprise part of the base or the denominator; but should that base or denominator include options and other rights that have not yet vested—*i.e.*, options and rights that cannot be exercised as of the time the earnings are determined?

Thus, *never* use a term of art. Take the time and make the effort to express the intent comprehensively and precisely.

* * *

Again (but probably not for the last time), a contract is a set of specifications for a transaction or business relationship, much like the specifications for the construction of a building or a bridge. If the specifications are inaccurate or incomplete ... well, that's welfare for the litigators.

H. Do not quit early.

Analogous to "terms of art" are statements which, in themselves, are correct but which are incomplete because they fail to specify terms required to apply their principles to circumstances that are likely to occur. Here is a simple example. A company sold its business and inventory. The buyer agreed to pay for the inventory as each item of inventory was sold. The contract, therefore, provided:

> Buyer will pay Seller, within ten (10) days after a sale by Buyer of any unit of the Inventory, the price for that unit as set forth in EXHIBIT B.

But when does a sale occur: on acceptance of an order?; on delivery and acceptance of the product? If the sale occurs on acceptance of the order, what happens if the customer refuses to accept delivery? The contract resolved these questions by providing in the next sentence:

> A sale of a unit of Inventory will take place on delivery and acceptance by a purchaser of that unit.

The buyer of the business would have to replenish inventory as it was sold. How did the parties determine whether the sale was of the seller's inventory or of the replacement inventory? The contract answered the question by specifying:

> All sales of products of the kind included in the Inventory will be deemed to be made <u>first</u> from the Inventory under this Agreement.

In contrast to the foregoing, the following provisions from an employee stock option plan are examples of an attorney's quitting too soon and not dealing adequately with the various considerations:

1. <u>Optionee's Right to Sell Option Shares to the Company</u>. Subject to the provisions of Section 3.04, upon written notice from an Optionee the Company shall repurchase at the Formula Price from such Optionee any Option Shares then owned by such Optionee which such Optionee wishes to sell....

2. Computation of Formula Price. The Formula Price shall be the highest [*sic*] of:

   (1) Fully diluted book value per Share; or

   (2) 7.5 times the weighted average of fully diluted net earnings (or loss) per Share over the preceding 3 years. In computing this weighted average the most recent year shall have a weighting of 4; the second past year a weighting of 2, and the third year a weighting of 1.

   However, no Option may have an exercise price less than the par value per Share at the time of grant.

3. Tax Provision. In computing the Formula Price, net earnings shall be after provision for income taxes, calculated as if the Company and its Subsidiaries filed separate consolidated federal income tax returns with the Company as the common parent.

The "put" to the company—*i.e.*, the requirement that the company, at the option holder's election, repurchase shares acquired under the option, should have been conditioned on the company's having adequate surplus to redeem the stock. Corporations, generally, may only purchase their shares from surplus; and when one option holder actually decided to exercise his option and sell the shares to the company, the company did not have any surplus, so the company was legally prohibited from honoring its contract.

What makes the oversight even more painful is that when the plan was prepared and adopted, the company's capital accounts were in deficit. A subsidiary concern that the plan also failed to address was the company's having some surplus but not enough to purchase all shares "put" to the company by two or more option holders. A simple parent company guaranty of the repurchase obligation would have solved the problem.

Other omissions, evident from the discussion of "terms of art", were (1) failure to define "diluted", (2) failure to exclude from the determination of after-tax earnings certain tax items (such as loss carry-forwards) occurring outside the relevant three-year period, and (3) failure to exclude from the determination of earnings extraordinary items of income or loss which are not in the regular course of the corporation's business. In addition, I doubt that anyone knows what "separate consolidated federal income tax returns" means.

The company, therefore, developed an alternate solution that did not involve the need for surplus, but it did require the draftsperson to deal properly with those omissions enumerated above. A version of that solution appears in Chapter 6A of *Commercial Agreements, supra*. It was developed with the aid of the company's accountants, as the original plan should have been.

* * *

As these examples attest, the draftsperson, often with the aid of the client or an expert in a particular field, must explore the various aspects of the transaction in order to identify those elements required to delineate the terms correctly and completely. Without this effort, the contract may fail to deal with situations that might likely arise, creating gaps that litigators fill with the mortar of their imaginations.

I. Do not use "et cetera" or its abbreviation "etc."

This term only creates an issue as to the items to which it relates. If a contract of sale reads: I sell you my house with the chairs, drapes, tables, etc., does etc. include the sofa, oriental rugs, free standing lamps, piano, artwork, etc.? The draftsperson must carefully examine the possibilities with the client and specify each item precisely.

J. Do not use the words "intend" or "intention" (as "... it is, therefore, the parties' intention that ..."); and do not use examples.

These terms and devices are unreliable braces for poor drafting. Intentions and examples rarely comprehend all possibilities. Like metaphors and allegories, they are often subject to different interpretations; and, of course, there is no one better to find an unexpected and unwanted interpretation than a good litigator. The draftsperson must forsake these faulty supports and expend the time and effort required to state a correct message.

K. Battle to avoid multiple negatives.

Multiple negatives convert the English language into a foreign language requiring translation. For example:

> It will not be inconvenient for the company not to refrain from not pursuing the matter.

Translation?

> It will be convenient for the company not to pursue the matter.

Multiple negatives make the message difficult to understand, thereby increasing the risk of error. Lawyers must train their minds to trigger a positive correction when they are writing in this negative mode.

L. Battle to avoid exceptions to exceptions.

Analogous to the use of multiple negatives is creating sentences with exceptions to exceptions:

> The company will not sell XYZ products in the State of New York other than in the Counties of A, B and C excluding the Cities of d, e and f in those counties.

Restated more exceptionally, the sentence might read:

> The company will not sell XYZ products in the State of New York, but the company may, nevertheless, sell those products in the counties of A, B and C, though not in the cities of d, e and f within those counties.

Or, in a more lawyeresque fashion, the revision might read:

> The company will not sell XYZ products in the State of New York, provided, however, that notwithstanding the foregoing, the company may sell those products in the counties of A, B and C but not in the cities of d, e and f within those counties.

Contracts are sufficiently difficult to write and to read. The lawyer should not create a puzzle to twist the mind needlessly.

M. Unwind.

Lawyers often combine in a single sentence two or more parallel ideas that require different treatments. The message is usually stated correctly but awkwardly as in the following example:

> Neither you nor I will write any article or other report for publication or give any speech or lecture concerning any of the experiments we conduct unless, in the case of an article or report, we do so jointly and with mutual agreement as to text, publisher and time of publica-

> tion, or, in the case of a speech or lecture, unless you and I agree on the text, the time and the audience, and credit.

It is usually better to house each idea in its own sentence. The separation lessens the danger of error by focusing on each concept independently and on the different treatment required for each, thereby providing the reader with a friendlier path to the ideas:

> Neither you nor I will write any article or other report for publication concerning any of the experiments we conduct unless we do so jointly and with mutual agreement as to text, publisher and time of publication.
>
> Neither you nor I will give any speech or lecture concerning any of the experiments we conduct unless you and I agree on the text, the time and the audience, and credit.

Before departing this topic, I must add one stunning example which illustrates not only the danger of combining parallel ideas but also the care required to avoid the agreement's becoming a nightmare for clients and a playground for litigators. A partnership agreement permitted the partners to engage in activities outside the partnership business. One partner engaged in outside activities, and a second partner sued the first for breach of his obligations, alleging that the activities interfered with the partner's duties to the partnership. The first partner, asserting that his conduct was proper, claimed indemnity from the partnership for his legal fees in defending the lawsuit based on a provision in the partnership agreement that read substantially as follows:

> The partnership will indemnify each partner for payments and liabilities incurred in the ordinary and proper conduct, or for the preservation of the business and assets of the partnership....

The partner claiming indemnity argued that the word "conduct" was not limited by the prepositional phrase "of the partnership", and that since his conduct was proper, he was entitled to indemnity. The other partner, of course, challenged this construction, maintaining that "of the partnership" modified "conduct". Had the draftsperson added a comma after the word "assets", this latter construction clearly would be correct; yet the better solution would have been to write the provision along the following lines:

> The partnership will indemnify each partner for payments and liabilities incurred in the ordinary and proper conduct of the partnership

> business or incurred for the preservation of the business and assets of the partnership....

Who was right, who was wrong, who prevailed are all irrelevant: The damage was already done.

Please see item 10.10 under Chapter 10 dealing with amendments to and rescission or cancellation of a contract.

N. Never do indirectly what you can do directly.

Lawyers are fond of short cuts, but shortcuts can be confusing; and confusion is but another siren beckoning the litigator. I have seen security agreements which state (A) that the collateral secures the borrower's obligations under the security agreement itself, and (B) that those very obligations under the security agreement also constitute additional indebtedness of the borrower under the borrower's promissory note. When I ask the draftsperson the reason for adding the obligations under the security agreement to the note, the usual reply is "That's the way we do it." Speculating on the origins of this bizarre provision, I offer the following Holmesian deduction:

> In the beginning, a lawyer in the firm was asked to prepare a security agreement for an already existing undersecured loan. The lawyer was careful and wanted to be sure that the existing collateral also secured the borrower's obligations under the new agreement. However, rather than amend the existing security agreement, the lawyer provided that the obligations under the new agreement would also constitute obligations under the borrower's promissory note, thereby gaining the benefit of the existing collateral already securing that note. The new agreement then became a form copied by other attorneys who did not question the applicability of these special provisions to their particular transactions.

A contract should not be a puzzle and should not require Sherlock Holmes to divine its meaning. In the example cited, each security agreement should provide that it secures (A) the loan, (B) the obligations of the borrower under the security agreement itself, and (C) the obligations of the borrower under the other security agreements. If amendments to existing agreements are necessary to accomplish the result, amend the agreements instead of trying to accomplish the result by some clever device which may not be understood or which may be overlooked because it is too esoteric.

O. Never incorporate one or more agreements into another agreement.

Sometimes the primary agreement in a transaction (for example, a loan agreement) will contain a provision incorporating subsidiary documents (security agreements) into it: For example:

> All of the Security Documents are incorporated by reference into this Agreement. If there is any inconsistency between any of the Security Documents and this Agreement, the provisions of this Agreement will control; but the Security Documents will be construed, insofar as possible, to avoid any inconsistency.

The provisions dealing with inconsistencies are defenses against poor writing. There should be no inconsistencies. If there are any, they are due to laziness and lack of care on the part of the attorney. More importantly, though, I find no reason for the incorporation of one agreement into another. Perhaps it is just a variation on doing indirectly something that should be done directly: a product of the relentless, mechanical copying of an obscure provision whose original purpose is lost somewhere in time.

On the other hand, incorporating specific provisions from one agreement into another, though burdensome to the reader, is acceptable:

> As used in this agreement, the terms A, B, C and D as defined in the Loan Agreement will have the same meanings in this Agreement.

However, whenever an attorney uses a shortcut such as this one, the attorney must carefully check the receiving document to determine whether any adjustments are needed to assure a proper fit. Except, perhaps, for the incorporation of defined terms, I prefer to bypass the shortcuts and draft the entire provision to suit the agreement for which it is intended.

P. Never include a provision that undermines another provision.

Most instances of this transgression occur in remedy clauses. The offending provision will state that before a party may begin an action, the parties must first try to resolve their differences amicably. Following is a typical example:

> If any dispute arises relating to this Agreement or any claim for damages is made as the result of breach of any obligation

> hereunder..., the parties shall use their best efforts to resolve such disputes through good faith negotiation. Each party shall designate representatives to conduct such good faith negotiations. Any dispute or claim for damages, as applicable, not resolved by such negotiation shall be resolved by arbitration as provided in Section 7.02 of this Agreement. [*sic*]

This particular clause presents two problems: first, an argument, albeit weak and bordering on the absurd, can be made that a party must first prove a breach in court before it can arbitrate the issue of damages; second, and more significantly, how long must the parties negotiate before one of them can bring an arbitration proceeding and what constitutes "good faith negotiations"?

The provisions requiring good faith negotiation should be excluded. Parties are always free to negotiate, and when a problem arises, they usually try to resolve their differences through discussion before resorting to litigation. If such a provision cannot be excluded, then the clause should be written along the following lines:

> If any dispute or claim arises relating to this Agreement, the parties shall use their best efforts to resolve such dispute or claim through negotiation, but at any time prior to resolution of the dispute or claim, either party may submit the matter to arbitration as provided in Section 7.02 of this Agreement.

See also, please, item 10.10 under Chapter 10, dealing with amending, rescinding and cancelling a contract.

Never give the litigator a platform—no matter how tiny it is.

Q. Never include in a contract a provision that you do not understand.

Sound silly? Witness this excerpt on the subject from a letter I received from Stephen E. Jenkins, a trial lawyer in Wilmington, Delaware:

> ... I have been shocked by the number of times in litigation that I have asked more senior lawyers—including some fairly good lawyers—to explain the meaning of some provision in a document they prepared and found out they had no idea what it meant. Indeed, I have just finished litigating one such case. The litigation did no one any good and would not have happened but for some sloppy drafting.

Enough said? Well, if not, then consider the reaction of a client to the answer, "I don't know", coming from the lawyer to whom the client is paying many hundreds of dollars an hour. I don't think the lawyer will be able to treat the matter as casually as Robert Browning. (See Chapter 3.)

R. Itemize.

To eliminate ambiguity, confusion and misunderstanding, itemize lists under distinctive subdivisions. For example:

Initial Draft:

(*You should not need a cryptographer to know what the words mean*)

The pertinent clause expressed the percentage component of a fee as

the lesser of 50% or the percentage interest in the profits or assets of the company, whichever is greater

Revised Draft:

The correction eliminated the pronoun, "whichever", expressing the percentage component of the fee as

(A) fifty percent (50%); or, if less,

(B) the greater of the percentage interest in the profits or the percentage interest in the assets of the company

* * *

And remember that statute in Maine which provided exclusions from overtime pay where a missing comma meant $5 million for the truckers. The exclusions were for

canning, processing, preserving, freezing, drying, marketing, storing, packing for shipment or distribution

Now see how itemization could have eliminated the ambiguity:

(1) canning, (2) processing, (3) preserving, (4) freezing, (5) drying (6) marketing, (7) storing, (8) packing for shipment or (9) distribution

S. And beware "and".

Be aware of the danger of using "and" in a sequence. Unfortunately, I have not found a court case dealing with "and vs. or"; but I hope the following examples and your awareness of litigators will convey the message.

Unacceptable:

The following will constitute a default: A, B, and C.

Acceptable depending on the intent:

The following, when existing at the same time, will constitute a default: A, B, and C.

Each of the following will constitute a default: A, B, and C.

Any of the following will constitute a default: A, B, and C.

The following will constitute a default: A, B, or C.

T. Oh, just one more.

State numbers in both words and figures: Twenty-three United States dollars (U.S.$23.00). Redundant? Yeah, but check out Chapter 5.

4.3 Conclusion

Surely there are more rules and techniques to improve drafting skills than those enumerated here, but in my experience these are the most important. In fact, I hope I have not tried your patience with too many, for it is never a good idea to overload the circuits. In any event, these guidelines are not a catechism to commit to memory. Indeed, I doubt that memorizing them would prove very helpful. Their function and the function of the examples and even (*horribile lectu*) the phantom stock plan in Chapter 6A of *Commercial Agreements* are to create awareness of what is involved in writing a contract. Once the lawyer accepts and assimilates the basic principle: A contract is the plan for a business transaction or relationship, and the prime directive: "Be accurate and as simple as possible", the lawyer will develop a sensitivity to the needs of the contract and to the language, a sensitivity that will dissolve the guidelines.... Thus, as we sail into the sunset, and before the dawn of a new chapter, I leave you with this lyrical remembrance of our journey.

WRITER'S RHYME

Word by word
line by line,
I'm gonna make
this writing fine.

I'll reread
'til I know
that each sentence
says it so.

Check the grammar
and the meaning;
be the critic;
do the screening.

Dictionary's
not for show:
Helps me get
those words to flow.

Watch the diet;
hem it in.
Do not fear
to make it thin.

Simple is
a goal to praise:
Let's untie
that wordy phrase.

Every word
let's be sure
follows the last
with meaning pure.

"Won't be easy,"
so 'tis said,
but effort will
put me ahead.

Word by word
line by line,
I'm gonna make
this writing fine,

even though
it takes some time,
I'm gonna make
this writing fine;

I'm gonna make
this writing fine.

Chapter 5

Proofread Assiduously

Every aspect of writing a contract is essential, even the most menial and boring such as proofreading. Lest there be any doubt, I offer the tragedy of the missing digits reported in an article by David Margolick that appeared in the October 4, 1991 edition of The New York Times.

When the financing for a fleet of ships was restructured and the new mortgage prepared, three digits were omitted from a crucial figure. Instead of the mortgage stating that it secured a debt of $92,885,000, it stated that it secured a debt of $92,885—not an insubstantial difference. Although this error appeared in almost 100 documents, none of the law firms that worked on the transaction, not even the mortgagee's in-house counsel, nor its out-house counsel, detected the error. Following the litigation, the mortgagee "reckoned that the typo had cost it at least $31 million".

"Didn't they proofread?!" you scream. Of course they did. What happened is a lawyer's nightmare, and what happened probably occurred because of one or two of the most common pitfalls in proofreading—the most boring of endeavors: (1) lack of concentration, and (2) the tendency of the eyes to see and the ears to hear what they expect rather than what is.

And this big little fiasco is the reason you should express numbers in both words and figures: twenty-three United States dollars (U.S.$23.00).

It is also helpful to take frequent, short breaks.

* * *

There is another aspect of Mr. Margolick's article that deserves attention. The article reports that the firm responsible for preparing the mortgage "knew the name of the erring secretary", whom the firm described as contrite and of unknown whereabouts. The implication that the secretary was to blame is outrageous. Secretaries type thousands upon thousands of characters an hour. No one knows how many errors will occur or how serious they will be; but everyone knows they will occur, as item 2 of Chapter 1 (**Les Preludes**) proclaims.

The person ultimately responsible for accuracy is the lawyer, not the secretary. By the time the document is presented for signature, "typos" do not exist; they have been superseded by proofreading errors and by "lawyeros". The lawyer must assume this responsibility—not drown it in the typing pool.

Chapter 6

There Is No Shame in Drafting a Fair Agreement

Too often lawyers—or, perhaps, just too many lawyers—believe that when they draft an agreement, they must prepare the document to reflect only the interests of their client. They pay little, if any, attention to the legitimate concerns of the other party.

I recall representing a client in the severance arrangements with his employer. The agreement, drafted by the employer's attorney, contained, as expected, a release by our client in favor of the employer; it did not contain a release in favor of our client. The agreement required our client to reimburse the employer for legal and other costs incurred by the employer to enforce the agreement. However, it did not contain comparable reimbursement provisions in favor of our client if he prevailed in the litigation; nor did it contain a provision absolving our client from the obligation to pay costs if he prevailed. Finally, the agreement gave the employer unilateral discretion to make certain determinations that could sever our client's rights to payment.

Highhanded drafting such as this is not only offensive, antagonizing the other party and the other party's lawyer, but it needlessly prolongs the negotiating and drafting process thereby adding to the legal costs of both parties and to the mounting lack of respect that clients and the general public have for lawyers.

In our comments to the employer's draft of the severance agreement, we added a release in favor of our client, we limited the discretion of the employer, we absolved our client from the obligation to reimburse the employer for the costs of enforcement if our client prevailed, and we added comparable reimbursement provisions in favor of our client. The results of these comments were mutual releases, limited discretion, and deletion of all provisions regarding costs of enforcement. These changes were made by the employer's attorney based on our counterproposals without any negotiation. (Related Assignment: Problem 16, *Exercises in Commercial Transactions*, second edition, Carolina Academic Press)

On another occasion, I received a draft of an agreement providing for the redemption by our client, on the East Coast, of the stock of a former employee located on the West Coast. In the most polite terms, the relationship between our client and the employee was strained, contentious, and devoid of trust. Yet, despite this atmosphere of distrust, not only did the attorney for the employee produce an agreement without the mandatory warranties that the employee's stock was free from any encumbrance, option or other right or claim, but the agreement failed to provide adequate assurances that on payment of the purchase price, the stock certificates, duly endorsed, would be delivered to our client. On this latter point, all that was needed was a provision for the employee's attorney to confirm (i) that the attorney had in its custody the duly endorsed stock certificates, and (ii) that the attorney would forward the certificates to our client on receipt of the purchase price in the attorney's escrow account.

* * *

The corollary to these observations, of course, is that consideration of the other party's legitimate concerns is also essential when commenting on the initial draft prepared by the other party. For example, in a financing that involved an assignment of charter hire to be deposited in a blocked account pending application to payments of principal and interest as they became due, the lender did not provide for interest while the funds remained on deposit. We drafted a clause providing for interest, which also took into account the lender's point of view. Following is the text of that clause:

> The Assignee will retain the funds that it holds in an interest-bearing account. The interest will constitute additional security for the Shipowner's Obligations, and while an Event of Default does not exist, the Assignee will, on each Repayment Date, pay the interest to the Shipowner to the extent it is not required for the payment [of principal and interest] due on the Repayment Date.

The lender accepted this text verbatim, thereby avoiding one or two steps in the drafting process, saving the client double legal fees for the time saved (since the borrower always pays the lender's legal fees[1]), and creating good rapport with the lender.

* * *

I do not know whether it is arrogance, indolence, naiveté, some other factor, or a combination of factors that compels an attorney to produce an agreement that assumes the attorney's client is the only party with a legitimate interest in the terms. Perhaps the compulsion arises from some recidivistic eruption of the medulla oblongata convincing the attorney that the attorney will create leverage in the negotiation by tilting the document excessively to favor the client. Perhaps it is the result of our adversarial training and the adversarial nature of the practice—at least insofar as litigation is concerned.

Agreements, though—all "agree"ments by definition—involve two or more parties trying to reach a common goal. True, as noted in Chapter 2, there is an adversarial aspect to the process of reaching agreement; but unlike litigation, there is also an element of commonality. Thus, as also noted in Chapter 2, an appreciation of and an effort to honor the legitimate concerns of the other party in the drafting process is essential—at least from this practitioner's point of view—to the efficient consummation of a transaction and the proper representation of one's client. In over fifty years of practice, I have yet to see one side either sustain an advantage by overreaching or "slip" anything by the other side. Invariably, the other party and its attorney—assuming relatively equal bargaining positions—will force the terms back to within the realm of reasonableness. The attorney, therefore, does not compromise the client's interest by preparing a fair agreement; in fact, by doing so, the attorney furthers that interest.

1. Well, not always. See "Poetic Justice" following Chapter 12 in *Commercial Agreements, supra.*

Chapter 6A

Controlling the Drafting

Well, if we learned one thing from the prior chapter, controlling the drafting is not about securing an edge. In fact, one good reason to produce the initial draft of an agreement or term sheet is to make sure that it is comprehensive and fair, taking into account the needs of your client as well as those of the other party.

But there are other reasons to produce the initial draft and any changes to that draft. The task of drafting those plans and specifications for the transaction, of necessity, requires the draftsperson to acquire a comprehensive understanding of the entire deal. From the beginning, that person will understand the transaction both on a macro and micro level better than anyone else. With that knowledge, there is less likelihood of overlooking something, some provision, some treatment, that should be part of the contract. Where the contract is concerned, it is better to be the draftsperson than—to mix a metaphor—to be a counter puncher.

* * *

It is also safer, much safer, to be the draftsperson for another reason. With so few exceptions that I can almost use the word "invariably", the initial draft of any contract will be changed. And amending an agreement is a tricky assignment as you will see in Chapter 8. In fact, as noted in that Chapter, I would rather write an agreement from scratch than amend one because a change to one part of the document often requires conforming changes elsewhere; and that very change requires an examination of the entire contract as well as any related documents. Knowledge of the entirety of the transaction, coupled with a detailed knowledge of the contract, minimizes the risk of oversight.

Chapter 7

Themes and Variations—Additional Suggestions

7.1 It Is Not Treacherous to Help the Other Guy

As observed at the end of the last Chapter, commercial transactions are not adversarial proceedings. The goal is not to win; the goal is to do a deal that conforms to the intent of the parties. Thus, while the attorney must at all times represent the interests of the client, the attorney must not seek to gain an advantage contrary to the terms of the deal from a mistake by the other lawyer. An obvious example—and surely one that begs correction—is the inadvertent omission of a word: "The Company will pay the following expenses ..." vs. "The Company will not pay the following expenses ...". Do unto the other lawyer as you would have that lawyer do unto you.

In the context of a commercial transaction, I doubt there is any better application of the Golden Rule than to the principle: Correct drafting errors of the other attorney. In fact, because the object of a contract is to reflect accurately the intent of all parties, I view this principle as an ethical mandate. Allowing errors that one detects to remain uncorrected serves two demons: a perverse desire to gain an improper advantage, and litigation that should never be spawned. The client is ill represented by that type of practice.

7.2 Be Aware of Your Limitations

The best philosopher of the Twentieth Century? Why Dirty Harry, of course: "A man has got to know his limitations." A while ago I was asked by an inventor to review the work of the law firm that was representing him in his acquisition from his former employer of patent applications for products that he had developed. The proposal by the former employer contained critical language restricting the inventor's right to develop certain products. The language was patent terminology, the meaning and implications of which neither I nor the other law firm understood. I, therefore, asked the inventor's patent counsel to review the language, and they suggested an important revision that permitted the client the flexibility he needed.

Recognition and acceptance of the limits of one's expertise are essential to represent the client properly, and if the required expertise does not reside within one's firm, the lawyer must obtain that expertise elsewhere. If the attorneys who drafted the stock option plan discussed in item H under Section 4.1 of Chapter 4 had consulted with the company's accountants, they might have corrected some of the errors. As mentioned in that Chapter, knowing our limitations, we developed the substitute arrangement with the aid of the accountants.

7.3 Do Not Wither within Your Area of Expertise

The corollary of knowing your limitations and finding assistance is knowing your strengths and using them. Often an experienced commercial attorney will have better perspective on a matter than the client or even a specialist. In these situations, the attorney should assume responsibility, and the attorney's judgement should usually prevail. Two examples follow.

As lead counsel for the development of a luxury condominium in Manhattan in the early 1980's, we retained special counsel to prepare the offering plan because our firm lacked expertise in that area. Their draft of the plan provided that interest earned during construction on deposits by the buyers would be credited against the purchase prices. I insisted that the provision be changed to pay the developer, our client, this interest without a credit to the buyers as long as the developer delivered the apartments in accordance with the sales contracts. Special counsel resisted, arguing that the attorney general had never approved—and so would never approve—a plan containing such a requirement. I countered that the attorney general would approve the plan as long as the interest arrangements were properly disclosed. "If the attorney general rejects the plan", I continued, "we will be in no worse a position." The minor delay and expense involved were well worth the potential reward.

The plan was submitted in accordance with my suggestion, and the attorney general approved it. At that time interest rates in the United States were the highest in recent history, so our departure from the norm meant substantial additional profit to the client. In fact, another developer, who was building a competing condominium at the same time and who had filed his offering plan prior to our filing, told our client that he had revised his plan based on ours and that because of the change he had made significantly more money. That developer was Donald Trump.

In the course of that same development, and in order to facilitate sales, our client wanted to obtain a commitment from a bank to provide mortgage loans to prospective buyers. The cost of the commitment would have been approximately $1,000,000, a substantial sum in that bygone era. I argued that anyone who could afford these condominium units would not need a mortgage or would be able to obtain financing without assistance, and, further, that any commitment would have so many contingencies and loopholes that it would be worthless. Nevertheless, the client persisted; but when we obtained a draft of the commitment and I revealed all the loopholes, the client relented and agreed to abandon the idea. Financing was never a problem in the sale of any unit. In fact, all sales contracts were signed without a financing contingency—that is, a provision that if the buyer was unable to obtain a loan, the buyer would be released from its obligation to purchase the apartment and the buyer's deposit would be returned.

Too often lawyers, even good, experienced lawyers, will present the various possibilities to the client, perhaps with a weak recommendation, but leave the decision to the client: "It's your money," the lawyer says, tucking the risk of responsibility under his tongue, "so it's your decision to make." On other occasions, a lawyer may allow a forceful client to override the lawyer's judgement, even though the lawyer is convinced the client is making a poor choice: "O.K.," says the lawyer, making the easy, safe choice, "the decision is yours." The choice, of course, is ultimately the client's: The client must decide whose judgement to follow. But the lawyer must not allow the client to make a decision that the lawyer believes is wrong without a forceful and effective presentation by the lawyer of the lawyer's position on the subject. When the matter is within the sphere of the lawyer's expertise, the lawyer must not permit the fear of being wrong to devour the lawyer's obligation to urge a course of action which the lawyer believes to be the best.

7.4 Respond Appropriately to the Other Party's Draft

There are four primary ways to respond initially to the draft of an agreement: by telephone; by a meeting; by a new draft; by noting changes to the original draft.

If there are only a few points that do not involve major issues or revisions, then response by telephone may be the most efficient way to reply. The lawyers can discuss the points and agree to any changes. To expedite the discussion, the person responding to the draft should prepare, before making the call, any suggested changes in wording.

A meeting is necessary only if there are major issues to discuss, but I cannot recall a situation in which I responded initially by calling a meeting. I would first give the other party written comments to clearly delineate the issues. This initial response provides the foundation and agenda for discussion, while allowing the other party to study your client's concerns without pressure to respond immediately, and, perhaps, to develop alternate suggestions to accommodate those concerns. It also reduces the risk of proposals being made in haste that have to be changed or withdrawn later because they were formulated without adequate consideration. In essence, producing written comments first will result in a more efficient and effective meeting.

I try at all costs to avoid rewriting the agreement and presenting the other side with a new draft. I doubt that anything infuriates a lawyer more than spending the time and effort to prepare a document only to receive a totally new document in reply. Even if the changes from the original draft are marked on the new draft, the attorney <u>must</u>, nevertheless, compare the new draft against the original to be sure the changes are correctly identified. Also, while it is relatively easy to focus on additions, the lawyer must return to the lawyer's original draft to understand deletions. In effect, the lawyer must now work with two documents. Thus, I only prepare a new draft—and it is rare that I do—if the original document is written so poorly that it defies comprehension or if the original document is entirely unresponsive to the needs of our client.

The way I usually respond to a draft, and the way I prefer to respond, is to mark deletions on the original draft and to add text by riders and handwritten inserts to that draft. This procedure gives the other side, in a single document, a comprehensive view of the issues and proposed solutions. It focuses and, therefore, facilitates discussion. Often the attorneys can resolve all or most of the problems by telephone, thereby narrowing the scope (and thus the cost) of any meeting that might be required. In most contractual matters, I find marking the changes on the initial draft the most effective, efficient response.

7.5 Presenting Drafts at a Meeting

Never, never, at a meeting, present a draft of a contract to the other party, asking that party to respond to the draft at that meeting! And never, never let anyone get away with pulling that maneuver on you!

I was asked by a major international corporation and its law firm to prepare a contract for a transaction which the company was desperate to do. After reviewing the contract with the client and the law firm, the client insisted that we have a meeting that day with the other party and its counsel at which we would present the draft, asking for comments. I said "No. You don't put anyone under that kind of pressure. We'll send them the contract today and schedule a meeting for tomorrow." Reluctantly, after a bit of friendly persuasion, the client relented. The next day we all met at my office and agreed on the contract in less than an hour.

On another occasion, my client was providing the financing needed to allow management to take a public company private. I was just a pup at the time. At the initial meeting, the high-profile, older attorney for the management team presented me with an agreement, stating emphatically that he wanted the document signed that afternoon. I, not too politely, returned the document to him, stating that we would not sign anything that day, and if and when we did sign anything, we would write it. His client immediately made him back off. When it comes to financing, money rules—at least until the loan is made. In due course the deal closed.

Always give the other party and its counsel time to digest.

7.6 Be Efficient in Preparing the Documentation

This word "efficient" appears quite often. It must be important. It is.

Unfortunately, lawyers who charge by the hour make money by inefficiency. But clients, ever more wary of legal costs, are becoming more demanding. At one point, our firm gained two new clients on recommendations because their former attorneys were inefficient and unresponsive.

Perhaps there are good lawyers ... even great lawyers who are not very efficient. But, as a general rule, to be a good lawyer, the lawyer must be efficient. And in the realm of commercial transactions, efficiency means organizing and ordering the various components of the transaction and vigorously pursuing them to conclusion. It helps to be compulsive; luckily most attorneys are. So

I need not attempt to solve the reader's insomnia with a treatise on efficiency. The key tool is located in Chapter 13: *The term sheet.*

In the realm that joins theory and practice, efficiency mightily serves the prime directive. No trickster induces error with greater frequency than pressure, requiring tasks to be performed more quickly than they should be. Efficiency diffuses that pressure, creating the mental space required to allow the mind to perform comfortably. The result is fewer errors.

As noted in Section 4.2, in over fifty years of practice, "time of the essence" has never been a factor or consideration in any transaction.

Just two more points: first, return phone calls and emails promptly—even, in the case of emails, at least to say something like "Noted. Thanks. Will consider and reply";[1] and second, don't wait until the last minute to attend to details that seem of minor importance, such as preparing and adopting corporate resolutions required to authorize the transaction.

7.7 Be Efficient in Dealing with Your Client: Meetings vs. the Telephone

As you well know, lawyers are fiduciaries: We have fiduciary duties to our clients. One of those duties, at least far as I am concerned, is to rein in our legal fees—regardless of student debt and other obligations, and regardless of material aspirations. "*IQ*", Integrity and Quality of Performance, will propel you to your financial goals.

---

1. Following is an email I sent to the Chairperson of the Law Review and the Dean of the law school I attended.

> Dear Chairperson,
>
> On October 24 [2017] I sent you the email that follows [omitted here]. I had little hope that the Law Review would act favorably on my request, but what disturbs me is that I have not received a reply from the Review—not even a "No" or a "Received and will revert." Common courtesy—and lacking that quality, common business sense—mandates a reply. To thrive in the world you will enter when you separate from the Harvard placenta requires more than academic skills. I thought that a simple reply to an email would not require a post graduate degree, but as Hemingway's character, Jake Barnes, said at the end of *The Sun Also Rises*: "Isn't it pretty to think so?"

I did not receive a reply to that second email, so I send a copy of it in reply to every solicitation for contributions that I receive from the law school.

The surest way to run up needless legal fees is to attend unnecessary meetings. You charge door-to-door time both ways and for the table banter that has nothing to do with the deal. If you must meet, meet at the lawyer's office. Instead, though, I urge that you use the telephone. *You and your client are discussing terms, concepts and strategies. There is rarely a need for a physical meeting to resolve these matters.*

I can't remember when last I met with a client to discuss a deal—certainly not in the last ten years. However, I do recall clients' asking me many times to meet with them at their offices. I tell them that we can handle everything in a fifteen minute telephone conversation or we can go through the costly ritual of a meeting comprising about three hours. Needless to say, we resolve the matters by telephone.

In fact, as noted in the prior section, there is rarely a need for lawyers to meet to negotiate terms of the contract. The results will be the same at less cost to the client using the telephone and the internet. I generally do everything by telephone, fax and the internet. Even complex transactions can be handled without meeting. I remember one large licensing deal many years ago, before the age of the internet, between parties in England and Japan in which I acted as special counsel to an English law firm and for which I wrote and negotiated the contract, coordinated local counsel in both countries, and closed the transaction in about a month without leaving my office, using the telephone, the telex (do any of you what device is?), and courier services.

As a general rule, play from your home ballpark.

7.8 Understand the Difference between the Active and Passive Voices; Know When to Use the Passive Voice

In the active voice, the subject of the verb performs the action:

John ate the frog.

In the passive voice, the subject of the verb is the object of the action:

The frog was eaten by John.

As a general rule, the passive voice should be used when the result of the action is the essence of the message and the doer of the action is either unimportant or unknown, or the person making the statement wishes to be vague:

The rain forests are being destroyed. We will perish.

Use the active voice when the action and the doer of the action are the important parts of the message:

> Pollution and urbanization are destroying the rain forests. We will perish.

Stylists prefer the active voice because the statements generally are shorter, more direct, and therefore more forceful than statements in the passive voice:

I shall cherish the gift always.

vs.

This gift will be cherished by me always.

However, in the contract, where loopholes are the enemy and the force of the statement is irrelevant, the passive voice is often the shorter and safer route to comprehensiveness. For example:

> If you damage the equipment, you will repair it.

But someone else might damage the equipment. Therefore:

> If you or anyone else damages the equipment,....

Still, lightning or falling rocks or an avalanche might damage the equipment. Thus:

> If you or anyone else or anything damages the equipment,....

Yet, what if the equipment is parked on a hill and the brake slips, and the equipment rolls down the hill into a mud pond fouling all of its parts? The last version should cover the situation, but I would not want to argue the point. So:

> If you or anyone else or anything damages the equipment or the equipment becomes damaged in any other manner,....

Or, more simply, use the passive voice when the result of the action is the essence of the message and how it occurs is immaterial:

> If the equipment is damaged, regardless of the cause,....

Another example? The passive voice is sometimes the better choice in default clauses:

> If a petition is filed by or against you in a bankruptcy or other insolvency proceeding and, if against you, it is not dismissed within thirty days,....

vs.

> If you file a petition in a bankruptcy or other insolvency proceeding, or if anyone files a petition against you in any such proceeding and the court does not dismiss it within thirty days,....

Sometimes the conjunction "if" or the verb "becomes" are signals to consider the passive voice. But the draftsperson must beware of the passive voice when the doer of the action is essential to the intended result. Thus, note the difference:

If the house is sold, I will pay you....

vs.

If you sell the house, I will pay you....

* * *

Perhaps in the contract, where the force of the statement is not important, the passive voice has greater use than in other forms of writing; but the draftsperson must not take this thought as an endorsement for the wanton use of the passive voice:

Passivable: The following services will be performed by you for which you will be paid by the company $______ per day....

Preferable: You will perform the following services for which the company will pay you $______ per day....

(Note: Despite the last example, this section has been sponsored by the Passive Voice Anti-Defamation League.)

7.9 Additional Tools

As a writer, the commercial lawyer should have two reference works to help implement the first half of the prime directive: a dictionary and a grammar handbook. I have both a dictionary and a grammar book at every desk that I use and by my bedside.

If you are not part of a law firm that has a varied practice with extensive form files on a wide range of transactions, populated by experienced attorneys to guide you, there is a third book, which normally modesty would enjoin me from suggesting; but, with Thornton Wilder as precedent (*Our Town*, Stage Manager, Act One), I will just mention it: *Commercial Agreements: A Lawyer's Guide to Drafting and Negotiating, supra.*

Chapter 8

Amending Agreements; Using Forms

Amending a contract, at least for me, is more difficult than writing the initial agreement because, frequently, changing even a single term of an agreement may require compensating or conforming changes to other provisions not only in the agreement that is being amended but in related agreements.

The addition of a new section to a contract illustrates the point. The sections that follow must be renumbered and the entire agreement and related agreements must be examined to correct cross references to those renumbered sections and to determine whether other changes are required because of the addition. However, you can avoid the tedious task of renumbering sections and checking cross references by simply numbering the new section to be added between sections 6 and 7, as section 6A. (Heck, I used that little trick when I added Chapter 6A to this book.) Nevertheless, as cautioned above, the lawyer must still examine the contract—*as well as any companion or related contracts*—to determine whether other provisions require change by reason of the addition.

To a certain extent, the computer will help. For example, if a defined term must be deleted from a contract, the computer will locate all uses of the defined term in order to delete them. But the task does not end there. The lawyer must then review the entire agreement to determine how to amend those provisions in which the defined term is used and to see whether other changes are needed because of the deletion.

* * *

The method of amending a contract also requires special care. Sometimes lawyers will amend a contract in the following manner:

> The agreement dated May 20, 2018, between A and B is amended to provide that B will....

This is a dangerous format and it should not be used because a general statement such as this may result in ambiguity and dispute: its effect on other terms of the agreement may be unclear. Instead, each provision affected by the change must be located and amended appropriately. The process amounts to a surgical procedure. The amendment should (1) revise the text of each provision to be changed, (2) state the effective date of the amendment and, if relevant, state whether the version of the agreement prior to its amendment will continue to govern any particular matters, and (3) confirm that the contract as amended remains in effect. For example:

> The agreement dated May 20, 2018, between A and B is amended, effective ___________, 2____, as follows.
>
> 1. The figure "$ X " in Section 3 of the agreement is deleted wherever it appears in that Section, and the figure "$ Y " is substituted in its place.
>
> 2. The second sentence of Section 4 of the agreement is amended in its entirety to read as follows:
>
> ____
>
> ____
>
> ____________________.
>
> 3. Following Section 5 of the agreement, a new Section 5A is added as follows:
>
> 5A. ____
>
> ____
>
> ____
>
> ____
>
> ___________________________.
>
> As hereinabove amended, the agreement will remain in full force and effect; but the agreement as it existed prior to the effective date of this amendment will govern those matters listed on Exhibit A hereto.

Many lawyers write the last sentence: "Except as hereinabove amended, the contract will remain in full force and effect." I do not know why they use that terminology, and I have never received a satisfactory explanation for its use. The word "except" seems to cancel the amendment or to place it in some amorphous state. Thus "As hereinabove amended, the agreement will remain ...", is the terminology to use.

Further, whenever a contract is amended, the writer must

A. Rewrite entirely each provision requiring change. Do not!!! amend by shortcuts like "The contract is amended to require Party A to do 'X, Y and Z.'"
B. Check the effect of the amendment on other provisions of the contact and on related contracts.
C. State the effective date of the amendment and identify any matters to be governed by the contract prior to its amendment.
D. Numbering—Adding a new Section between Sections 6 and 7. Don't add a new section 7. Instead add a new Section 6A. This avoids the need to renumber and to check cross references.

* * *

Finally, commercial lawyers are plagiarists, but not in an illegal or evil sense. Precedents, forms and models that treat a particular transaction are useful and necessary tools. But they must be used with caution. The same principles and discipline required to amend a contract must be applied to the use of a form. Like snowflakes, no two transactions are identical. Thus, no matter how basic a provision may seem, the lawyer must examine it carefully to determine whether changes are required to adapt it to the particular deal.

The danger in using a form is adopting the text without critical examination. Forms prompt laziness and dull the defenses. The lawyer must be alert to these dangers and must be aware that a form will not fit a transaction just by completing blanks or substituting alternate clauses. Using forms is like buying ready-made clothes: They usually require alterations. If the form fits precisely, the fit is purely by coincidence. Writing a contract cannot be reduced to a practice by numbers. If it could, little need would remain for the commercial lawyer.

And please, please do not be seduced by the promises of AI. It will be a long, long time, if ever, before the silicon chip can out think the carbon based unit. The chip lacks the imagination, the flexibility, the experience, and the insight to assess and adapt to the differences and nuances that exist between transactions that seem to be alike.

* * *

Amending a contract is a demanding exercise that the lawyer must execute diligently in order to avoid error. And that same diligence must be applied to the use of any form or model.

Related Assignment

Problems 6, 7 and 20, *Exercises in Commercial Transactions*, Second edition, (Carolina Academic Press)

KAY*
(A Prelude to Part II)

Each man a time.
Each man a place.
He understood.
It eased the way.

But use the time
and use the space.
None better than he,
none with more grace.

There were no maps, no proven ways,
so most would stand and safely graze.
Though always some might see the chance,
only he could make us dance.

He filled the vessel
with dreams they called,
but when he poured
pure wine was all.

So now remember, remember when
he caught the sun for us to play.
His time he used, he used his place,
and we found fortune in his grace.

---

* Kay Sugahara was and will always be one of the great entrepreneurs.

Part II

Contract Basics; Basic Terms; Basic Agreements

Chapter 9

Structure of Contracts; Preambles; Definitions; Covenants

From that title, it appears we have much to discuss here, eh? Well, we don't! I'll do my best not to waste your time.

9.1 Structure of the Contract

Like the members of the human race, contracts come in a grand variety. And as the human race itself differs from all other species, contracts, as noted in Part I, differ from all other forms of writing. You can take all the sections of a contract, throw them in the air, and reassemble them in any order you wish: The contract will have the same meaning as it did when those sections were in their original order. You can't do that with a brief or an essay, or a novel, a poem or a play.

In fact, the standard dictionary definition of a contract, "a legally binding agreement between two or more competent parties", is wrong. There are many <u>enforceable</u> contracts to which only one person is a party. These contracts are often referred to as unilateral agreements. The best example is a promissory note, which is signed only by the obligor of the debt evidenced by the note. Another example is a guarantee, which is usually signed only by the guarantor. And confidentiality agreements, where only one party is receiving confidential information, are usually signed only by that one party.

Even the standard conception of a contact: "AGREEMENT dated the __ of ________, 2___, between...." is not universal. Often a contract is written in the form of letter agreement:

> This letter will confirm the agreement between you and us as follows: ...

The only essential ingredients to all contracts are that they be supported by "consideration" and that they conform to the law, and those are elements about which, I trust, you learned in your contracts course.

9.2 Preambles

Preambles are statements that introduce the actual agreement. They are not essential. Generally, promissory notes, guarantees, and confidentiality agreements do not contain preambles. In other agreements, preambles usually appear as "WHEREAS" clauses that, like an introduction, precede the actual agreement. They describe the foundation and nature of the transaction and contain definitions of terms that will be used in the operational part of the contract. "WHEREAS" clauses should <u>never</u> contain any operating term ("I will do X, and you will do Y") of the agreement. They should be limited to stating the background of the deal.

9.3 Definitions

An example of a defined term appears in Chapter 11, where, for the purpose of brevity, I say that I will use the word "warranty" to refer to both representations and warranties. Definitions are tools useful to avoid the necessity of repeating lengthy, sometimes complex language. The most common example is defining the parties to a contract as, for example, "Lessor" and "Lessee" in a lease. An example of definitions for more detailed information appears below. The example is from a preamble to a license of intellectual property.

> WHEREAS, Licensor has developed certain computer programs which contain data bases that the Licensor has assembled and compiled, all as listed on Exhibit B to this Agreement (collectively called the "Computer Programs", and the data bases contained therein are separately called the "Data Bases")....

The defined terms eliminate the need to use, throughout the agreement, lengthier references as, for example, "the computer programs, including data bases, listed on Exhibit B to this Agreement", and "the data bases listed on Exhibit B to this Agreement".

Defined terms usually begin with a capital letter in order to identify them throughout the agreement. Remember, though, as cautioned in Chapter 4, that if you choose to refer to the same, undefined concept in different parts of the contract, you must use the same language in all places lest you create an ambiguity.

9.4 Covenants

You don't need me to explain what a covenant is. A good dictionary will do the job. But in case you don't have one at hand, a covenant is simply a promise or commitment to do or not to do something ("I will do X; you will do Y; and neither you nor I will do Z"). The purpose of agreements is to create legally enforceable covenants. Of course, the nature of the covenants depends on the nature of the transaction, and crafting them requires the care and dexterity discussed in Part I in order to avoid unintended consequences.

Take a moment to scan the Table of Contents of *Commercial Agreements, infra*, in order to get an idea of the vast number and variety of deals that populate the commercial world, each of which requires covenants as well as other provisions styled to fit the transaction. The Table of Contents is available on line without charge, as is the Topical Index.

9.5 Supporting Cast

As the main characters in a dramatic work have a supporting cast, so do the main covenants in a contract. You will meet many of these supporting players in Chapters 10, 11 and 12.

Take, for example, a license of intellectual property. The primary covenants are (1) the grant the license or right to use the IP, (2) the term of the license, and (2) the promise by the licensee to pay a fee or a royalty for that right. In a loan agreement, the primary covenants are (1) the lender's promise to make the loan, and (2) the borrower's promise to repay the loan with interest. These primary covenants comprise the core or, if you will, the plot of the contract.

As noted above, the supporting cast in these agreements will include, among others, many of those common clauses discussed in Chapter 10, and representations, warranties and indemnities discussed in Chapters 11 and 12. But, depending on the nature of the transaction, clauses that might appear to be basically the same such as representations and warranties, can differ significantly in purpose. So, for example, the representations and warranties in a license agreement attest to the integrity of the intellectual property that is the subject of the license. Hence, in a license agreement, the representations and warranties are always accompanied by indemnities that protect the licensee against any of those properties violating or infringing the rights of another, thereby jeopardizing the right of the licensee's use of the property and the business based on that use.

On the other hand, the representations and warranties in a loan agreement attest to the credit worthiness of the borrower and the integrity of any collateral securing the loan. Thus, in a lending transaction, a breach of a representation or warranty will give rise to a default allowing the lender to "call", or demand immediate payment, of the loan. Here there is generally no need for indemnities.

So, as discussed in Chapter 2, and before committing you to the material that follows, recall that the job of the transactional attorney is to think first in terms of the various considerations involved in each transaction, then in terms of how to treat each of these considerations, and finally in terms of writing the words to embody those decisions.

* * *

Resource Materials: Structure; Preambles; Definitions; Covenants

The following materials supplement the teaching in this Chapter. They are available on Westlaw to law students and their teachers without charge if the law school has a plan with Westlaw that includes *Commercial Agreements, infra.*

> *Commercial Agreements—A Lawyer's Guide to Drafting and Negotiating*, Thomson, Reuters
>
> (Just note the formats. Content will always vary according to the transaction.)
>
> Chapter 2: Unilateral contract (promissory note)
>
> Chapter 2B: Formal contract—preambles (WHEREAS clauses), definitions
>
> Chapter 6B: Letter agreements
>
> Any of the Chapters above: Plot and supporting cast

Chapter 10

Common Clauses (Boilerplate)

10.01 Introduction

The provisions discussed in this chapter are considered "boilerplate", which a cynic would define as "experience encrusted by time and sustained by fear". As I hope will be evident from the first two discussions (termination and assignment clauses), the lawyer must chip away the crust, contain the fear, and examine these provisions carefully to determine whether they apply to the particular transaction and, if so, how they should be crafted to assure a proper fit.

Many of the samples that follow are shorter than comparable provisions found in current commercial documentation. Nevertheless, they are comprehensive and do the job intended; but, as noted above, each requires careful consideration to determine whether it is appropriate and whether it requires adaptation.

Of course, if all of the provisions discussed in this chapter are included in the contract, there will be little room left for the important provisions specifying the terms of the deal. The attorney, therefore, must use his or her judgment to determine whether a particular type of provision is appropriate.

10.02 Termination

Provisions respecting termination of a contract require special attention, lest there be room to argue that rights and obligations that should survive termination have also terminated. I use the word "argue" because rights and obligations that are clearly of a kind intended to survive termination should, in fact, be enforced by the courts following termination. The art, though, is to avoid the courts; so the careful draftsperson will consider the effect of termination clauses on the various other parts of the agreement. Stated another way, the draftsperson will identify those provisions which should survive termination and provide for their survival. Common examples are warranties, indemnities, and non-compete provisions found in agreements such as employment contracts and licenses. Thus, in contracts such as these, provisions granting the right to terminate should usually state that this right is a right to terminate "the employment" or "the license"—not the contract itself. As an added precaution, attorneys often add a sentence along the following lines:

> The provisions of this section shall survive termination of [the employment/the license/the agreement].

The danger, though, with adding a sentence such as this to one section, is that it must now be added to all sections that should survive, lest a negative implication be drawn as to those sections from which it is omitted. An alternative would be to include in the agreement a separate section listing all those provisions that survive termination.

Other types of agreements, such as those for finders, sales agents and brokers, require special attention and negotiation with regard to transactions that might close after termination or expiration and for which a fee should be payable. In these cases, a provision along the following lines is appropriate:

> This agreement will remain in effect until ______________. Termination will be without prejudice to the rights and obligations of the parties accrued to the date of termination, and following termination this agreement will continue to apply to, and the fee under Section ___ will be payable with respect to (i) any contract signed on or prior to termination, and (ii) any contract signed after termination on which you were working prior to termination or which is with a party you introduced to us prior to termination.

Please see item 10.10 below dealing with amendments to and rescission or cancellation of a contract.

10.03 Assignment

Another provision which requires special attention is the assignment clause. As a general rule, parties to a contract do not want to deal with anyone else—at least not without their approval. Landlords are especially guarded about tenants subletting or assigning the lease for fear that the tenant, if it decides to quit the premises in a rising market, will get the benefit of the increased rental value. Similarly, a licensor of intellectual property will not want a licensee to transfer the license or sublicense the property lest the licensor lose an opportunity for a further license.[1]

But prohibitions against assignment can be a nuisance—and even an impediment—when a party wishes to sell its business or to sell the division to which the contract belongs, or if it wishes to merge or consolidate with another company. The impediment becomes even greater when the contract provides that a default will occur if control of a party to a contract is transferred.

Though not endless, the types of assignment clauses are certainly numerous. A comprehensive clause might read along the following lines:

> Neither party (a "Transferor") may transfer or assign any of its rights or obligations under this agreement without the prior written consent of the other, and any such transfer or assignment or attempt thereat will be null and void. A change in control of a party or of any entity

---

1. See Chapters 10 and 10A of *Commercial Agreements*, *supra*, regarding license agreements.

> that controls a party, either directly or through one or more other entities, in a single transaction or series of transactions, will constitute a transfer. "Control" means the ability, either directly or through one or more entities, to control or determine the management of an entity, whether by election of those members who can determine the decisions of the board of directors or other governing body or by contract or any other means. A change in control may, without limitation, occur by merger or consolidation regardless of the surviving entity.
>
> In the case of any transfer or assignment permitted by this section, the Transferor will remain liable for the performance of all of its obligations under this agreement regardless of whether those obligations arose before or arise after the transfer or assignment.

Sometimes it is appropriate to permit transfers to a successor to a party's business as, for example, in the case of a lease of equipment. A clause to that effect might read as follows:

> Neither party may transfer or assign any of its rights or obligations under this agreement without the prior written consent of the other, and any such transfer or assignment or attempt thereat will be null and void; provided, however, that either party (a "Transferor") may, without the consent of the other party, transfer and assign its rights and obligations under this agreement to any corporation or other entity which succeeds by merger, consolidation or purchase to all or substantially all of the business and assets of the Transferor and which assumes all of the obligations of the Transferor under this agreement. In the case of any transfer or assignment permitted by this section, the Transferor will remain liable for the performance of all of its obligations under this agreement regardless of whether those obligations arose before or arise after the transfer or assignment.

Of course, the possibilities are many, but the foregoing should provide guides for any desired variations.

10.04 Governing Law

Almost every contract contains a governing law clause, even contracts which do not need one such as those between two parties located in the same jurisdiction to be performed in that jurisdiction. Generally, the law chosen to govern the agreement must bear a reasonable relationship to the contract: usually to the location of one of the parties, or to the place of performance, or to the place where the contract is made. New York, though, with certain exceptions, permits non-New York parties to select New York law to govern their agreement regardless of the relationship that the agreement bears to New York, provided the transaction involves at least $250,000. For transactions involving at least $1 million, New York, again with certain exceptions, permits non-New York parties to maintain actions in the New York courts which relate to agreements governed by New York law regardless of the relationship that the agreements bear to the State.[2]

The party with the leverage—such as a bank making a loan—usually selects the governing law. Rarely is the choice of law clause the subject of great debate. Although, like most lawyers, I prefer the law of my own jurisdiction to govern, unless there is some special concern, I will yield to the other side's preference of almost any of the United States in situations of relatively equal bargaining position. However, as advised in Chapter 15, it is wise to consult counsel outside of your jurisdiction—especially if there is a matter of special concern.

The choice of law clause is quite simple:

> This agreement will be governed by and construed in accordance with the law of the State of ______________.

To avoid any risk that the chosen state will, through some perversity, under its conflicts of law rules, thwart the parties' choice and apply the rules of another jurisdiction, some lawyers will add after "... law of the State of ________" a statement along the following lines: "as it applies to contracts made and performed wholly within that State." However, on choice of law clauses, my paranoia and irrationality end with "construed in accordance". And to that very point, the New York Court of Appeals (New York's Highest Court) in IRB-Brasil Resseguros, S.A. v. Inepar Investments, S.A., 20 N.Y. 3d 310 (2012) stated that "an express exclusion ... of New York's conflict-of-laws rules is not necessary." In arriving at this decision, the Court cited the Restatement (Second) of Conflict of Laws, Section 187, that states "[i]n the absence of a contrary indication of intention, the reference [to the law of the state chosen by the parties] is to the local law of the state of the chosen law."

* * *

A few other points regarding the choice of law are worth noting. Often a party with leverage such as a lender will require the other party to submit to

2. New York General Obligations Law Sections 5-1401 and 5-1402. Please see Chapter 15 dealing with multi-jurisdictional transactions.

the jurisdiction of courts with a specified venue. Sometimes, though, a situation arises in which parties about to enter into an agreement are at odds about the governing law and the location to determine disputes. A consideration possibly more important than the governing law, and one which might well contribute to the disagreement—especially in the case of small companies—is the cost and inconvenience of being sued in a foreign jurisdiction. One solution is to provide that the party asserting a claim must bring that claim in the jurisdiction of the other party and that any counterclaims which the other party might have at the time must be brought in that same law suit. A compromise such as this might even provide—to the dismay of the litigators—a stimulant to settle disputes.

Please see *Commercial Agreements, supra*, Chapter 2 (submission to jurisdiction), and §16X:21 (dual jurisdictions, scheduled to be included in the 2028 Supplement). Mr. Siviglia will be happy to furnish teachers with a copy of that Section. Teachers may contact him at psiviglia@aol.com.

10.05 Arbitration

As a general rule "shallow pockets" prefer arbitration and "deep pockets", especially when contracting with "shallow pockets", prefer the courts. When representing an employee under an employment contract, I always try to include an arbitration clause.

Also as a general rule, arbitration forecloses access to the courts to resolve disputes. So in contracts containing both arbitration clauses and provisions for injunctive relief respecting matters such as the protection of trade secrets, confidentiality, and competition, the agreement should contain a clause to the following effect to allow access to the courts in order to seek equitable relief:

> Notwithstanding the provisions for arbitration contained in this agreement, [specify party] will be entitled to injunctive and other equitable relief in the courts as provided in this agreement and as the courts may otherwise determine. In any such proceeding [specify party] will not be required to post bond or other security.

Following is a sample arbitration clause for arbitration under the rules of the American Arbitration Association. The provision for entry of judgment is essential to confirm the award, at least in the Federal courts, (9 USCS §9).

> Any dispute or claim arising under or with respect to this Agreement will be resolved by arbitration in [specify venue], in accordance with

> the Rules for Commercial Arbitration of the American Arbitration Association before a panel of three (3) arbitrators, one appointed by _[x]_, one appointed by _[y]_, and the third appointed by said Association. The decision or award of a majority of the arbitrators shall be final and binding upon the parties. Any arbitral award may be entered as a judgment or order in any court of competent jurisdiction.
>
> The scope and extent of discovery will be determined by a majority of the arbitrators in accordance with the rules of the American Arbitration Association, or if there are no rules governing discovery, then the scope and extent of discovery will be determined by a majority of the arbitrators.
>
> The entire proceeding or portions of the proceedings may be conducted via a remote, virtual medium as determined by a majority of the arbitrators.
>
> Each party will bear its own legal fees and the fees of the arbitrator that it appoints. The parties will bear equally the fees of the American Arbitration Association and the of the arbitrator that it appoints.

One further point regarding arbitration: If a party's performance under a contract with an arbitration clause is guaranteed, then the guarantee should contain a provision as set forth below to avoid the need for a separate lawsuit on the guarantee. The first two sentences are essential, for unless the guarantor is a party to the arbitration proceeding, an award will not be rendered against it. The last sentence preserves the beneficiary's options.

> The undersigned agrees to become, and without further act shall be, party to any arbitration proceeding under the Contract. The undersigned shall not appoint an arbitrator in any such proceeding. The undersigned shall be bound by any award rendered in any such proceeding, and any award rendered against the Obligor under the Contract and in favor of the Beneficiary under the guarantee shall also be rendered against the undersigned and in favor of the Beneficiary and may be entered as a judgment or order in any court having jurisdiction. Notwithstanding the foregoing provisions of this paragraph, and in addition to those provisions and regardless of whether an arbitration proceeding is pending under the Contract, the Beneficiary may at any time enforce its rights under this guarantee in any court of competent jurisdiction.

10.05A Mediation

Mediation is an attempt—before submitting a dispute to arbitration or the courts—to resolve the dispute, which parties themselves have been unable to resolve. The parties present their positions to an impartial mediator, who then tries to develop and negotiate a mutually acceptable compromise.

I prefer to avoid this additional layer of dispute resolution, relying on the parties and their attorneys—confronted by the cost, delay, aggravation and divisiveness of litigation—to develop a mutually acceptable solution. After all, as noted in the Closing Comment to Chapter 23:

> good negotiators must also possess the qualities of skilled mediators.

If, however, the parties wish to include mediation as part of their deal, following is a form for such a provision:

> Either party may, by notice to the other party, propose to submit any matter in dispute to mediation. The other party shall then, by notice to the party that made the proposal, accept or reject mediation.
>
> If the parties agree to mediation, they will submit the matter for mediation in [*Specify Venue*], under and in accordance with the Commercial Mediation Rules of the American Arbitration Association (the "AAA"). The AAA will appoint the mediator, who will be knowledgeable about the subject matter of the dispute.
>
> The entire proceeding or portions of the proceedings may be conducted via a remote, virtual medium as determined by the mediator.
>
> Each party will bear its own legal expenses, and the parties will share equally the charges of the AAA, any other costs of the proceeding, and the fees of the mediator.
>
> Either party may, at will, terminate the proceeding at any time before the parties sign an agreement settling the dispute.
>
> If a party rejects mediation or terminates the preceding, either party may [*As Applicable: submit the matter to arbitration as provided in this agreement // commence a legal proceeding with respect to the matter*] and/or pursue any other rights and remedies that it has.

10.06 Recovery of Legal Fees

Contracts sometimes contain a provision requiring the losing party in a litigation to pay the legal fees of the winner. I have a problem with provisions of that kind, for it is not always clear who is the winner and who is he loser. For example, Party A sues Party B for $250,000 but is awarded $25,000. Who won—especially if Party B offered $50,000 during settlement discussions?

As an alternative, I would provide for the reimbursement of legal fees and other costs that a party incurs only in the case of a frivolous claim or defense asserted by the other party. Please see § 16X:12 of *Commercial Agreements, supra.*

10.07 Notice

Notice provisions can needlessly overwhelm a contract, to wit:

> Any notice, communication or demand to be given or made by or to _[x]_ or _[y]_ pursuant to this Agreement shall be in writing and shall be given or made by prepaid registered or recorded delivery airmail letter or by telex, telegram or cable (confirmed by pre-paid registered or recorded delivery airmail letter) addressed and sent to _[x]_ at:
>
> ________________________
> ________________________
> ________________________
> ________________________
>
> Telex: ____________________
> Answerback: ________________
>
> and to _[y]_ at:
>
> ________________________
> ________________________
> ________________________
> ________________________
>
> Telex: ____________________
> Answerback: ________________
>
> or to such other addresses and telex numbers as _[x]_ and _[y]_ respectively may notify to each other. Any such notice, communication or demand if given or made by registered or recorded delivery airmail letter shall be deemed to have been received when actually received but not later than seven (7) days after the same was posted and in proving such it shall be sufficient to prove that the envelope containing the same was properly addressed and posted as aforesaid and if given or made by telex shall be deemed to have been received at the time of dispatch.

This clause is from a contract that I reviewed for a client. Not only is it absurd in its detail but, remarkably, it provides for notice by telex and not fax ... a bit of fossilized experience I would say.

Given the modern means of communication and the uncertainty of the mails, I opt for a simpler provision. It states that notice will be deemed given on receipt or, if the other party insists, delivery (in this context I see no difference between the two because the sender can choose the manner of communication and can easily verify delivery). Further, the preamble to the agreement will contain the addresses and fax numbers of the parties, eliminating the need to repeat them in the notice clause. I avoid notice by email because, unlike a fax, there is no confirmation of delivery. Also, I limit the clause to "notices", as there may be many informal "communications" under an agreement (as, for example, by telephone to check on the delivery date of an order) for which the formality of a notice clause would be inappropriate. Following is an example:

> Notices under this agreement shall be in writing and sent to each party at its address or fax number set forth above or, in the event of a change in any address or fax number, then to such other address or fax number as to which notice of the change is given. Notices to [X] will be sent to the attention of ____________ or to such other person as to whom notice is given. Notices to [Y] will sent to the attention of ____________ or to such other person as to whom notice is given. Notice will be deemed given on receipt.

10.08 Execution and Counterparts

Counterparts are identical copies of the same document. Following is a counterpart clause from an actual agreement. It is a collection of unnecessary words signifying nothing.

> This agreement may be executed in several counterparts each of which shall be deemed to be an original, and all such counterparts when taken together shall constitute one and the same instrument.

The only time a counterpart clause is necessary is when all parties cannot sign the same copy. The clause, then, should read along the following lines:

> This agreement may be executed in any number of counterparts. It is not necessary that all parties sign all or any one of the counterparts,

> but each party must sign at least one counterpart for this agreement to be effective.

Sometimes it is inconvenient for parties to sign an agreement together at the same time and place. Instead of circulating counterparts—and especially when there are only two parties to the contract—execution can be easily effected by facsimile exchange. In fact, I signed the contract for *Commercial Agreements* in this manner. Here's the clause:

> This agreement may be executed and delivered by exchange of facsimile or PDF copies showing signatures of _[x]_ and _[y]_, and those signatures need not be affixed to the same copy. The facsimile or PDF copies showing the signatures of _[x]_ and _[y]_ will constitute originally signed copies of the same agreement requiring no further execution.

10.09 Authority to Contract and to Sign

Agreements will sometimes contain warranties by the signatories that they are duly authorized to sign the contract on behalf of their respective parties. The agreement will end with a meaningless flourish along the following lines:

> Each of the persons signing below warrants that the person is duly authorized to sign this agreement on behalf of the party for which the person is signing.

A warranty of this kind is worthless. The authority either exists or it does not exist. The statement that authority exists when it does not will not, through some chemistry of the written word, create the authority. "But," you say, "at least if the person signing does not have the authority, we can sue the signatory for breach of warranty." By the very act of signing, the signatory warrants that authority. A separate statement to that effect is redundant. Besides, if the client has to sue the signatory on breach of warranty to sign, the client's lawyer has blown his or her assignment.

Generally, there is no problem as to the authority to sign. Within three months after a subsidiary breached its contract with my client, the client collected over $8 million under the parent company's guarantee signed by a Vice President of the parent without board action. No issue was raised as to authority. The consideration for the guarantee was clear. But, if there is a question as to authority, resolutions of the directors and a certificate of authority as to the signatories should be required. See Chapter 16 of *Commercial Agreements, supra.*

10.10 Amendment; Rescission/Cancellation

A. Amendment

Requiring amendments to be in writing is one provision I never—at least I hope I never—omit from any contract:

> This agreement may be amended only by an instrument in writing signed by the parties hereto.

B. Rescission and Cancellation

Sometimes combining ideas that require different treatments is so easy that the mind, unless it pauses, will fail to detect the trap. For example, as noted above, a common and important provision in written agreements is the clause dealing with amending the agreement:

> This agreement may be amended only by an instrument in writing signed by the parties hereto.

A natural impulse might be to add the concept of cancellation or rescission:

> This agreement may be amended, rescinded or cancelled only by an instrument in writing signed by the parties hereto.

However, contracts often have termination clauses. Sometimes one or both of the parties have the right to cancel the contract at specified times or on the occurrence or failure to occur of certain events. Even in the absence of such provisions, a party generally has the right to cancel the contract if there is a material default by the other party. Thus, a provision dealing with rescission or cancellation by written agreement should be treated separately from the provision dealing with amendment. For example, and depending on the content of the agreement:

> Except as otherwise provided in this agreement and without prejudice to the rights of either party on default by the other, this agreement may be rescinded or cancelled only by an instrument in writing signed by the parties.

10.11 Waiver

Requiring that waivers be in writing is also another worthwhile clause:

> Neither party may waive any of its rights or any obligation of the other party or any provision of this agreement except by an instrument in writing signed by the party charged with the waiver.

10.12 Delay in Enforcing Rights

Provisions dealing with delay in enforcing rights are closely related to waivers. They are particularly important in promissory notes, guarantees, security agreements and other financial instruments. Following is an example:

> The failure or delay by [either party] in enforcing any right or obligation or any provision of this agreement in any instance shall not constitute a waiver thereof in that or any other instance. [Either party] may only waive any such right, obligation or provision by an instrument in writing signed by it.

I will not argue the philosophical difference between "delay" and "failure" in this context, except to note that at some point, "delay" can become "failure", so the use of both words is correct and has purpose.

10.13 Remedies

The purpose of these clauses is to allow a party the greatest flexibility in enforcing a contract and to avoid any requirement in the law respecting election of remedies that might apply in the absence of these provisions. These clauses are invariably found in financial documents and are important where the lender has several options as, for example, against the borrower, against a guarantor, and against collateral. Each of the agreements—the loan agreement, the guarantee, and the security agreement—should contain a provision dealing with the subject. Following is an example:

> The rights and remedies provided in this agreement are cumulative and not exclusive of any rights or remedies provided by law or by any other agreement. The exercise by _X_ of any right or remedy will not preclude _X_ from exercising any other right or remedy. _X_ may pursue its rights and remedies in such order as it determines.

10.14 Integration Clauses

These clauses provide that the agreement supersedes all prior dealings between the parties relating to the contract. Their purpose is to exclude those prior dealings from having any legal effect and from their being used as evidence as to the meaning or intent of a particular provision. Some attorneys include them automatically in every contract. I do so when I think the provision is appropriate. However, I destroy all prior drafts, even though I cannot require the other side to do so. Following is a form of this type of provision:

> This agreement contains the entire understanding of the parties with respect to the subject matter of the agreement, and it supersedes all prior understandings and agreements, whether written or oral, and all prior dealings of the parties with respect to the subject matter of the agreement.

10.15 Expenses and Interest

Expense clauses are still another type of provision found mostly in financing documents. They usually cover expenses of negotiating and preparing the documents and of collection. Following is a fairly comprehensive provision:

> The Borrower will reimburse the Lender for or at the request of the Lender will pay: (a) expenses (including, without limitation, reasonable legal fees and disbursements) incurred by the Lender in connection with the negotiation and preparation of this Agreement and the other [Loan Documents] and in connection with the transactions contemplated by this Agreement and the other [Loan Documents]; and (b) expenses (including, without limitation, reasonable legal fees and disbursements, court costs and the cost of appellate proceedings, and any other reasonable costs of litigation) incurred by the Lender in connection with (i) enforcing, preserving, defending and perfecting any right and any security interest under this Agreement or any of the other [Loan Documents], (ii) protecting and collecting any of its collateral, and (iii) any proceeding respecting any of the foregoing.
>
> The Borrower will pay the Lender interest at the rate of ___% *per annum* on any amount which the Borrower owes to the Lender under this Section: (i) from the date the Lender expends the amount in any case where the Lender has requested the Borrower to pay the same

> and the Borrower has failed to do so within three (3) business days, or (ii) from the date the Lender requests reimbursement in any case where the Lender has not requested the Borrower to pay the same.

10.16 Severability

Severability provisions are designed to protect (i.e., avoid frustration of) the contract in the event a provision of the agreement is unenforceable. They are usually included in contracts where one party has a powerful bargaining position and requires that the contract include some harsh terms that may not be enforceable. They are found in leases and mortgages, and they are also included in employment agreements because of the provisions relating to competition and equitable remedies. Following is a typical example:

> If any provision of this agreement or the application of any such provision to any person or circumstance is held invalid, the remainder of this agreement, and the application of such provision other than to the extent it is held invalid, will not be invalidated or affected thereby.

10.17 Section Headings

As a regular matter, agreements with sections that contain titles also contain a section vitiating any effect of those titles. These provisions are appropriate because a label used merely for convenience to locate or identify a particular clause should have no bearing on the interpretation of the operative language of the agreement. A typical provision of this kind will read as follows:

> Section headings are for reference purposes only and shall not in any way affect the meaning or interpretation of any provision of this agreement.

* * *

Well, that's it for me. I trust you've had enough too.

Chapter 11

Representations and Warranties; Due Diligence

Any discussion of representations and warranties requires a concomitant discussion of due diligence, for reliance on any representation or warranty without conducting the proper due diligence amounts to risky business.

11.1 Representations and Warranties

A. Preliminary Analysis

Though there is a legal distinction between a representation and a warranty, as a practical matter the distinction is not significant because of the way contracts are written. A representation is generally considered a statement to the recipient in order to induce the recipient to enter into a contract, so a breach could give rise to an action for termination or rescission of the contract. A warranty is a statement that generally will only give rise to a claim for damages. The reason this distinction is not significant is that (1) the contract will usually comprehend both by stating that PARTY A "represents and warrants" to PARTY B, and (2) the contract will also usually state the remedies for a breach of a representation or warranty. Yet because of that legal distinction between a representation and a warranty, some contracts, like those for the purchase of an automobile or other equipment, will use only the word warranty.

Now, having dispensed with some legal niceties, let's get down to what's important.

* * *

A representation or warranty is a statement of what should be true, either at the moment the statement is made ("our financial statements are accurate and complete"), or at sometime in the future ("our work will be without defect in material or workmanship"). Whether the statement be a representation or a warranty, what is certain is that the party on the receiving end is relying on the statement when signing the contract. And as Polonius ironically observed that "brevity is the soul of wit" (*Hamlet* II, ii), and also in the interest of the environment, henceforth I will use just the word "warranty".

Warranties will vary depending on the type of transaction to which they relate. For example, the warranties of the seller of a business will differ from those of a licensor of intellectual property, and the warranties of a builder or manufacturer will differ from those of the seller of a business and a licensor of intellectual of property. The crucial warranties of the seller of a business relate to such matters as the financial statements, litigation, contracts, and intellectual and other properties owned by the business. Warranties of the licensor of intellectual property will relate primarily to the ownership of that property and to its not infringing upon any other intellectual property or violating the rights of others. And the key warranties of a builder or manufacturer will relate to the quality of the product—that there will be no defect in material or workmanship or, when appropriate, in design.

As you may have noted from the preceding paragraph, there may well be overlap between the warranties of the seller of a business with intellectual property and the licensor of intellectual property. Other standard warranties will also overlap, such as the agreement's constituting the legal, valid and binding obligation of a party and its not violating any other agreements binding on that party. But the essential point to remember and to execute properly is to tailor the warranties to the particular transaction. And, as you will note from the Resource Materials at the end of this Chapter, the transactions are many and varied.

Vital to remember is that the way a transaction is structured can make a difference on the effect of a warranty. Take, for example, the acquisition of a business. There are three ways to accomplish an acquisition: purchase the business and assets of the company; purchase the stock of the company; merge the target company into the acquiring company.

- In the case of an asset purchase, the buyer will suffer direct injury if warranties respecting the assets prove to be incorrect. So, if there is a breach of warranty respecting, say, intellectual property, the buyer, itself, will have a claim against the seller for the devalued worth of that property caused by that breach.

But, in the case of an asset purchase, the seller may liquidate and dissolve following conclusion of the sale. So the buyer should insist on a guarantee of the warranties by the shareholders or should require other security, such as an escrow of a portion of the purchase price, in case of a breach. Any guarantee or other security should secure the indemnities (indemnities are a topic treated in Chapter 12).

- In the case of a stock acquisition, the result is different: The "devalued" property remains an asset of the company being acquired, which has no claim because of the breach, while the buyer's injury is indirect: The buyer would have to prove a loss in value of its investment, which would be a more difficult loss to prove. A refinement for buyers to consider is to require the warranties and indemnities to run not only in favor of the buyer but also in favor of the company that is being acquired. A provision to that effect **must**—lest knowledge of a fact vitiate a claim based on that fact—be accompanied by a clause stating that knowledge by the company being acquired of any matter will not impair any of the warranties in its favor or any of its rights and remedies and that the company being acquired will, in addition to the buyer, be entitled to enforce the warranties and indemnities as if it were the buyer.

  A further refinement would be to merge the company that is being acquired—*i.e.* the target company—into the buyer or into a subsidiary of the buyer, with the representations of the target's shareholders, who are being bought out, running directly to the surviving entity. This arrangement results in the warranties having the same effect as those in an asset purchase because the beneficiary of the warranties is the surviving entity which, by virtue of the merger, acquires the assets of the target.

- In the case of a merger in which the shareholders of the participating companies become shareholders of the surviving entity, the result would be the same as an asset acquisition **provided** the participating companies merge into a new entity, and their shareholders give the warranties to that new, surviving entity, and, if desired, to each other.

  If, on the other hand, the surviving entity is one of the companies participating in the merger [as opposed to a newly-formed company into which they are merged] and the participating companies give warranties to one another, then the warranties would be meaningless because in a merger the participating companies become one and the same, resulting in no remedy, since the surviving company would be suing itself.

These differences do not mean that all business acquisitions should be asset purchases, since there are many more considerations involved in an acquisition as you will see in Chapter 19. But these differences and Chapter 19, itself, illustrate distinctions of which attorneys must be aware and which attorneys must assess to determine the best way to accomplish a transaction.

B. Disclaimers and Limitations

Contracts will often contain disclaimers of warranties, limited warranties, and limitations on damages. You may even have experienced a limited warranty in the purchase agreement for your automobile, and you may have noticed that the dealer who sold you the automobile disclaims all warranties, relegating you, the buyer, to the manufacturer's warranties. In any event, when dealing with contracts for the sale or lease of equipment or other goods, you must consult the following statutory provisions:

> for sales UCC § 2-105 (definition of goods), and §§ 2-313 through 2-316 (express warranties, implied warranties, and the exclusion or modification of warranties), and
>
> for leases UCC § 2A-103 (definition of goods), and §§ 2A-210 through 2A-214 (express warranties, implied warranties, and the exclusion or modification of warranties).

Since a warranty is a statement of something that is supposed to be true, makers of warranties sometimes try to dilute the warranty by adding qualifiers such as "to our knowledge" or "to the best of our knowledge". Qualifiers like these often appear with respect to warranties pertaining to whether intellectual property that is being purchased or licensed infringes or violates the rights of others. Of course, the buyer or licensee wants a clean, unqualified warranty lest the seller or licensor, to avoid liability, seek refuge inside the qualification ("We didn't know"). Often the result will depend on the importance of the warranty to the buyer or licensee, the confidence of the seller or licensor in the truth of the warranty, and the negotiation.

In certain circumstances, a blanket disclaimer of any warranties may be appropriate. As noted above, dealers, who are merely links to a market and have no part in the production of the product, will disclaim making any warranty. Under an option granting the lessee the right to purchase equipment leased to it under a net lease, where the lessee is responsible for the care, maintenance and repair of the equipment, the owner will make no warranties with respect to the equipment, requiring the lessee to purchase it "AS IS". However, the owner will warrant that it is the owner of the equipment, that the sale does not violate the rights of anyone else, and that the equipment is free from any liens or claims arising out of acts or obligations of the owner or out of the equipment itself (*e.g.*, defects).

Again, treatment depends on the situation: how important the warranty is to the buyer or licensee; how confident the seller or licensor is in the warranty; and the negotiating positions of the parties. (See Chapter 23 on negotiating.)

C. Statute of Limitations

As a general rule, the statute of limitations with respect to a warranty begins to run from the date the warranty is made unless (i) the warranty relates to a future performance, and (ii) discovery of a breach of that warranty must await the time of such performance. See UCC §2-725(2).

For example, warranties made to a buyer of loans, such as the buyer of a package of mortgage-backed securities, relate to matters as they exist at the time of the sale. Usually there is no warranty that the loans purchased will perform in the future without default. Hence, the statute of limitations on warranties relating to the sale of loans will generally begin to run from the date of the sale.

In 2016 a New York appellate court, relying on decisions of New York's highest Court, addressed the issue of whether a clause tolled—that is, suspended the running of—the statute of limitations on breach-of-warranty claims made in respect of loans purchased as part of a mortgage-backed securities package.[1] The clause in question stated that any cause of action relating to a breach of representations or warranties

> shall accrue as to any Mortgage Loan upon (i) discovery of such breach by the Purchaser or notice thereof by the seller to the Purchaser, (ii) failure by the Seller to [cure, repurchase or substitute] and (iii) demand upon the Seller by the Purchaser for compliance with this Agreement.

In holding that the clause did not toll the statute, the Court, in a unanimous decision, stated the "clear rule that a breach of contract claim in [a residential mortgage-backed securities] put-back action accrues on the date the allegedly

1. Deutsche Bank National Trust Company v. Flagstar Capital Markets Corporations, (App. Div., 1st Dep't.), 53 N.Y.S. 3rd 252, 29 NY 3rd 986, 75 N.E. 3rd 669.

false representations and warranties were made." The court went on to state: "[W]e find that the accrual provision is unenforceable ... because it is premised on extending the statute of limitation", which, at least in New York, is "against public policy".

In effect, the underlying premise of the clause was a breach of warranty [item (i) of the clause] pertaining to matters existing at the time of the purchase. The clause failed to target a "future performance", such as a default by a borrower following the closing.

The lawyers for the buyer may have been guilty of malpractice for not knowing the law or for failing to navigate safely within the law, but, ironically, a claim for malpractice may have been barred by the statute of limitations.

A relatively simple solution would have been a provision along the lines of a credit default swap, which is an insurance policy against default and so is keyed not to the date the warranty is made but to the date of a future event: a default. In effect, the swap gives the holder of the swap the right to put or sell the debt back to the seller. The Resource Materials at the end of this Chapter cite Section 16X-17 in *Commercial Agreements* that offers two models for this type of solution.

11.2 Due Diligence

You may recall that I mentioned a short while ago (depending on how fast you read) that the party receiving a warranty is relying on that warranty when signing the contract. Well, don't let your client rely too heavily on the warranties, especially in the acquisition of a business.

Due diligence is the investigation that a party conducts to assess whether to enter into a deal and on what terms—especially in the case of the acquisition of a business. That sounds like a responsibility of the buyer, right? Well, not always. If the seller is receiving anything other than the entire purchase price in cash—say stock, or debt, or cash plus stock and/or debt—the seller is also a buyer and must conduct its own due diligence. An acceptable alternative to all cash would be some cash and deferred payments represented by a negotiable promissory note secured by an irrevocable letter of credit issued by a prime bank.

An article that appeared in the June 15, 2012 Business Section of *The New York Times* illustrates the point. "Goldman Sachs and the $580 Million Black Hole" recites a horror story spawned by the failure to conduct proper due diligence into the buyer's financial condition. The article reports that the sellers, an elderly couple, James and Janet Baker, with little experience in transactions of this kind, retained Goldman Sachs as their investment advisor. The article also reports that Goldman Sachs was to conduct due diligence.

The buyer's initial offer to the Bakers was $580 million, half in stock, half in cash. The final price, which the Bakers accepted, was $580 million all in stock. Within six months after the deal closed, the company went into bankruptcy. The article reports that the buyer had falsified information about its customers and its sales, fallacies that the Goldman personnel assigned to the project failed to detect.

In case your client is not convinced by the Baker debacle, you can explain that even audited financial statements can't be trusted. In 2012 Hewlett-Packard announced an $8 billion write down because of accounting errors by a company that H-P had acquired. The errors occurred prior to the acquisition.

And just to be sure there is no doubt, Chapter 22, "Over Lawyering, or How to Lose a Deal", provides a stunning example of how the failure to conduct any due diligence resulted in a major developer's loss of a prime construction site in Manhattan, while the application of some simple, obvious due diligence allowed another developer to "steal" the opportunity. When studying that Chapter, please observe the effect due diligence had on the indemnity respecting the warranties favoring the winning buyer.

Proper due diligence is a hedge, and as Chapter 22 proclaims, it can also be a weapon. It is well worth the time and the cost. And that cost should be considered the premium for an insurance policy.

Resource Materials: Warranties; Due Diligence

The following materials supplement the teaching in this Chapter. They are available on Westlaw to law students and their teachers without charge if the law school has a plan with Westlaw that includes *Commercial Agreements, infra.*

> *Commercial Agreements—A Lawyer's Guide to Drafting and Negotiating*, Thomson Reuters.

Mr. Siviglia will be happy to furnish teachers with materials not yet published. Teachers may contact him at psiviglia@aol.com.

- § 16X:11: **Due Diligence**
- Chapters 6E, 6F and 6G dealing with Real Estate Construction Contracts
- Chapters 10 and 10A: License agreements
- Chapter 10B: Development of a product

- Chapter 11: Stock acquisitions, including notes 5 and 7 regarding limitations
- Chapter 15: Asset acquisitions
- Chapter 15.1: Sale of equipment by a manufacturer
- Chapter 15C: Disclaimers under financing leases
- Chapter 15E: Construction of capital equipment (to be added by the 2026 Supplement)
- Chapter 15F: Purchase of used capital equipment (to be added by the 2027 Supplement)
- §16X:17: Warranties and the Statute of Limitations (to be added by the 2028 Supplement)

Chapter 12

Indemnities

Indemnities are like insurance policies: they provide protection for a party to an agreement against the risk of a breach of that agreement by the other party. But, like insurance policies, an indemnity depends both on how well the coverage is written and the credit worthiness of the indemnitor. In some cases, the contract will require the indemnifying party to obtain "contractual liability insurance", which, essentially, guarantees performance by the indemnitor of its obligations under the indemnity. And when the indemnitor is a subsidiary, a parent company guarantee of the entire contract may well be in order.

Like warranties (Chapter 11), indemnities must be styled to the particular transaction, with their scope often depending on the negotiation.

You might well ask: "Why does a contract need an indemnity provision. Aren't the risks of breach covered by the law of damages?" Yes, they are to a certain extent. But the indemnity provides precise protection, eliminating any ambiguities or uncertainties in the law, and, in some cases, they cover some damages that the law might not cover as noted in the analysis that follows.

The typical indemnity provides protection against (i) loss and damage, (ii) liability to third parties, and (iii) expenses that a party might incur because of the breach. In addition to requiring reimbursement of legal costs, most indemnities also require the indemnifying party to provide the indemnitee with legal defense against third party claims arising from the breach, which generally is not a requirement of the law.

Indemnities most often partner with warranties. For example, in the case of a breach of warranty by a licensor to the effect that the intellectual property licensed does not violate the rights of anyone, the licensee

(i) may sustain damages for the cost of—and the loss of profit from—product that it has produced but that it cannot sell,

(ii) may be liable for improper use of intellectual property owned by the third party claiming the infringement of its property, and

(iii) probably will incur expenses such as litigation costs, not only for claims by the licensee against the licensor (generally not covered by the law or the indemnity),[1] but also for claims against the licensee by the third party claiming infringement.

But indemnities also partner with other kinds of breaches. As Mr. Jaggers (in Charles Dickens' *Great Expectations*) might say: Let me "put this case." A real estate developer that does not have its own construction company will engage a contractor to perform the construction. If there are flaws in the construction, or if the contractor in performing its work causes damage to others, the indemnity will protect the developer against

(i) the cost to correct the errors,

(ii) claims by third parties for damages caused by the contractor or by the errors in construction, and

(iii) litigation costs.

Indemnities can protect against many kinds of breaches. However, the indemnity should protect not only against an actual breach but it should also protect the indemnitee against claims asserted against the indemnitee even if there is no breach: *that is, claims containing allegations which, if true—regardless of whether they are true—would constitute a breach.* If the indemnity covers claims such as those, then the indemnitee will not have to prove a breach in order to collect litigation costs incurred to defend against the claim. Further, if the indemnitee settles the claim, the indemnitee will not have to bring a separate action against the indemnitor to prove a breach when seeking to recover the amount of the settlement. The rationale for this broader coverage is that the claim asserted against the indemnitee arises solely out of the conduct of the indemnitor and not because of any fault of the indemnitee. Further, in the case of indemnities respecting warranties, the party making the warranty, which, in essence, is a statement of what should be true, should assume full responsibility for any claim against the indemnitee containing allegations that contradict the warranty.

---

1. See Chapter 10, item 10.06, dealing with recovery of legal fees.

As a matter of fairness, though, the indemnity should also include a provision that the indemnitee will not settle a third party claim against it without the indemnitor's consent (i) unless the indemnitee releases the indemnitor from its obligation of indemnity in respect of that claim or (ii) if the indemnitor, providing defense against the claim, ceases to provide that defense or is in default in any of its other obligations under the agreement.

Further, as noted in Chapter 11 dealing with warranties, in the case of an asset acquisition of a business, the buyer should require a guarantee by the shareholders or other security such as an escrow of a portion of the purchase price to secure the indemnities because the seller may liquidate and dissolve following conclusion of the sale.

And one final note: As a general rule, litigation costs incurred to enforce an indemnity are not recoverable from the indemnitor. So it is wise to include a requirement that the indemnitor pay the costs that the indemnitee incurs to enforce its rights to indemnity.

These and other aspects of indemnities are treated extensively in the Resource Materials cited below.

Resource Materials: Indemnities

The following materials supplement the teaching in this Chapter. They are available on Westlaw to law students and their teachers without charge if the law school has a plan with Westlaw that includes *Commercial Agreements, infra.*

> *Commercial Agreements—A Lawyer's Guide to Drafting and Negotiating*, Thomson Reuters.

Mr. Siviglia will be happy to furnish teachers with materials not yet published. Teachers may contact him at psiviglia@aol.com.

- Chapters 6E, 6F and 6G dealing with Real Estate Construction Contracts
- Chapter 10: License agreements
- Chapter 10B: Development of a product
- Chapter 11: Acquisitions, including notes 5 and 7 regarding limitations
- Chapter 15.1: Sale of equipment by a manufacturer
- Chapter 15C: Equipment leases, including disclaimers and limited warranties and contractual liability insurance

- Chapter 15E: Construction of capital equipment (scheduled to be added by the 2026 Supplement)
- Chapter 15F: Purchase of used capital equipment (scheduled to be added by the 2027 Supplement)
- § 16X:17: Warranties and the Statute of Limitations (scheduled to be added by the 2028 Supplement)
- Chapter 3: Guarantees

Related Assignments

Problems 28 and 29, *Exercises in Commercial Transactions*, Second edition, (Carolina Academic Press).

Chapter 13

Building Agreements—Term Sheets vs. Letters of Intent

Both letters of intent and term sheets are detailed outlines of the terms of a proposed transaction. The difference between the two is that letters of intent are signed by the parties contemplating the transaction while term sheets are not signed.

Each, the letter of intent and the term sheet, is a useful tool to vet a transaction to be sure that the parties agree in principle before moving to preparing the contracts. And initial drafts of each can provide excellent tools for the lawyer to vet the proposed deal with the client before proceeding with a draft for all parties to examine.

Appearing below is the only form of letter of intent I will allow a client to sign:

That's right, I will not allow—and I have never allowed—a client to sign a letter of intent. They are the fibers from which litigators weave their suits.

Although the letter of intent is a universally accepted form, in the myriad deals that I have done over more than 50 years, the lawyers for the other parties have always agreed, without protest, to proceed using a term sheet instead of a letter of intent.

Though letters of intent proclaim vociferously that they do <u>not</u> constitute agreements and that they do <u>not</u> create any obligations, do not underestimate the ability of hungry litigators to locate and devour prey. In fact, at the same time I was writing a portion of *Commercial Agreements, supra,* dealing with this very topic, my law firm was also involved in a claim based on a letter of intent, which had been signed before the client came to our firm. And you may recall (or, in the case of you younger folk, you may be aware) that in 1985 a jury rendered a verdict of $10.5 billion against Texaco for interfering with an agreement between two other oil companies, which, according to both of those oil companies, was just an agreement in principle *subject to* the signing of a definitive contract. That judgement forced Texaco to seek protection in bankruptcy.

Lest you think that I am overreacting, Philip D. Beaumont of the prestigious New York law firm, Chadbourne & Parke, in a review of *Commercial Agreements* which appeared in the May 24, 1994 issue of the *New York Law Journal*, agreed with me:

> His recommendation, in Chapter 11, to avoid letters of intent at all costs is also sound.

* * *

What then is the alternative to a letter of intent? Instead of a letter of intent, my clients and I use a term sheet to vet the essential elements of the transaction. As noted above, the term sheet is not signed. It is simply an outline.

After preliminary discussions between the parties to determine whether there is mutual interest in proceeding, I will prepare a term sheet setting forth the conditions of the proposed transaction. When we have a draft that my client approves, we give that draft to the other party. The term sheet provides transparency, allowing the parties to focus on and to understand easily the essentials of the deal without having to wade through the dense text of a contract. It facilitates the discussions.

Once the parties agree on the term sheet, we prepare the contracts. Since the business terms have been resolved, the negotiations on the contracts, themselves, are generally swift and painless. They are limited, for the most part, to clarifying details and refining the text.

I recall using this procedure on a $100 million financing for a real estate project. (At that time $100 million was a lot of money.) After we had agreed on the term sheet, the lawyer for the lender lamented: "You guys negotiated so hard on the term sheet, I dread the negotiation on the loan documents." "Don't worry," I replied, "there'll be no problem with those." After everyone had approved the loan documents, the lender's attorney said to me, "Peter, you were right. They went smoothly and quickly." I must admit, though, I did have to restrain my younger partner from overnegotiating a few points.

Resource Materials: Term Sheets

The following materials supplement the teaching in this Chapter. They are available on Westlaw to law students and their teachers without charge if the law school has a plan with Westlaw that includes *Commercial Agreements, infra.*

Commercial Agreements—A Lawyer's Guide to Drafting and Negotiating, Thomson Reuters.

- Chapter 2B: For a loan
- Chapter 11: For a stock acquisition
- Chapter 15: For an asset acquisition
- §16X:14: For purchase of less than 100% of a company

Related Assignments

Problems 11 and 19, *Exercises in Commercial Transactions*, second edition, (Carolina Academic Press).

Chapter 14

Confidentiality Agreements

14.1 Preliminary Analysis

A confidentiality agreement, as the name implies, protects the secrecy of proprietary information that one party discloses to another. Confidentiality agreements also contain a second, essential protection: they restrict the other party's use of the information, lest an unwanted use of the information dilute or destroy its value to the owner.

(Often lawyers and business people refer to these instruments as "NDAs" or Non Disclosure Agreements.)

Confidentiality agreements are used in a variety of situations:

- for employees, especially in hi-tech companies, to protect information that they will necessarily encounter or develop in doing their jobs;
- in contracts to develop a product where parties share their proprietary information in order to create the new product;
- in acquisitions to protect information disclosed to the potential buyer while that potential buyer conducts its "due diligence" investigation into the company that it is seeking to acquire;
- for threshold discussions between parties to explore the possibility of a transaction or business relationship between them such as the license or purchase of intellectual property.

There is no question as to the necessity of a confidentiality agreement when parties *must* share information to develop a product or in some other form of joint enterprise. Nor do I question the advisability or appropriateness of these agreements for employees, even though the law, itself, enjoins employees from misappropriating the trade secrets and other confidential information of their employers. However, I have serious reservations about a confidentiality agreement for the purpose of discussions between parties to explore a possible transaction or business relationship and during the due diligence period of a possible acquisition.

As my clients began to call more and more frequently for confidentiality agreements to cover exploratory discussions, and to send me drafts prepared by the other party to review, I became more and more skeptical. I have always advised clients that these agreements, no matter how well written, are, at best, weak instruments because of the difficulty to prove breach and damages. Again, the only sure winners will be the lawyers.

At the exploratory stage, especially in the case of intellectual property, the only important thing that has to be disclosed is what the technology or the process or formula or other trade secret will do—not how it is put together or what makes it work. When I asked my clients what they planned to disclose and whether my observation was correct, invariably they replied that at this stage of the discussions there was no need to disclose any technology or other trade secret. So I told them: "Don't sign a confidentiality agreement. Don't be lulled into a false sense of security. Save the legal fees. Just be sure not to disclose anything that you wouldn't want someone else to use." The clients agreed, and so did the other parties with whom they planned to discuss the transactions.

Here is the actual advice I gave. Please note the admonition in the second paragraph:

> As I mentioned in my voice mail, I consider confidentiality agreements for purposes of discussing possible business arrangements worthless. You must assume that anything you disclose will be used in a manner that you do not want.
>
> Thus, even if a confidentiality agreement is signed, you must not disclose any of your technology or any of your other proprietary or confidential information. You should always limit disclosure to what you and your products can do; you must not disclose what makes them work or how they are put together.
>
> If this mandate is followed, a confidentiality agreement is not necessary. (Just think of the legal fees the company will save.)
>
> If the other party insists on a confidentiality agreement, then it is all right to sign one as long as you follow the mandate.
>
> We have a standard form of confidentiality agreement if you still require one. I plan to go fishing in the morning, but will be back in the office about 3 p.m. Texas time.

Heck, can you imagine Coca Cola disclosing the Coke formula under a confidentiality agreement?

14.2 Two Types of Confidentiality Agreements

Confidentiality agreements come in two forms. One requires the party making the disclosure to mark or identify as confidential and subject to the agreement any material or information that it deems confidential. The other assumes that all materials and information disclosed are confidential unless otherwise specified or unless they fall within one of the permitted exceptions, which are discussed below.

The advantage of the first is precision; its disadvantage is the risk of forgetting to identify a disclosure as confidential. The advantage of the second is that, by being all-inclusive, it avoids the risk of oversight. For that reason, I prefer the second format, but either format is acceptable.

14.3 Specific Provisions

Confidentiality agreements contain exceptions and limitations, most of which must be viewed cynically and should be rejected or stringently qualified. Unfortunately, those exceptions and limitations are too often accepted "as a matter of course", without challenge.

A. Term

A confidentiality agreement *must never*, though many versions do, contain an expiration date. A secret is forever! Even if you can you imagine Coca Cola entering into a confidentiality agreement concerning the Coke formula, can you imagine it doing so with an expiration date on the requirement of confidentiality?

B. Absolute Mandate

The obligation of confidentiality must be absolute. Mandates that require the recipient of information to protect that material in the same way that it protects its own secrets are unacceptable because (A) the recipient's methods of protection may not be adequate, and (B) if there is a leak and the recipient's methods of protection were followed, the disclosing party is damaged but is without remedy against the disclosee and may well be burdened by litigation to protect against the use of that information by others.

C. Exceptions

The exceptions to the requirements of confidentiality must be crafted with great care. The universal exception is information that is in the public domain: hardly a necessary exception, for if the information is in the public domain, it ain't confidential. But we paranoid lawyers always include it anyway.

Other common exceptions are for prior knowledge, for information developed independently, and for information received from someone else. Too often confidentiality agreements merely recite these last three without appropriate qualifications. I will include the first (prior knowledge) with appropriate proof of that knowledge delivered promptly, but I resist the last two: information developed independently (Ha, not likely after disclosure), and information received from someone else.

If absolutely necessary to include either or both of the last two (information developed independently and information received from someone else), they must be qualified by appropriate proof that must be delivered prior to any use or disclosure, and any use or disclosure must await a specified period following delivery of the proof.

Resource Materials: Confidentiality Agreements

The following materials supplement the teaching in this Chapter. They are available on Westlaw to law students and their teachers without charge if the law school has a plan with Westlaw that includes *Commercial Agreements, infra.*

> *Commercial Agreements—A Lawyer's Guide to Drafting and Negotiating*, Thomson Reuters.
>
> - Chapter 16, including note 2.5 on corralling exceptions
> - Chapter 11: Acquisitions

Chapter 15

Multi-Jurisdictional Transactions[1]

The Need for Local Counsel Notwithstanding a Contract's Governing Law or Anything Else

15.1 The Background

In December 2012 the New York Court of Appeals (New York's Highest Court) rendered its decision in IRB-Brasil Resseguros, S.A. v. Inepar Investments, S.A., 20 N.Y. 3d 310 (2012). The case involved a conflict of laws issue to which the court applied Section 5-1401 of the New York General Obligations Law. That Section permits parties to a contract involving at least $250,000 to select New York as the governing law.

The case concerned a suit to enforce payment under a guarantee issued by a Brazilian guarantor. The guarantee contained a New York choice of law clause.

Under Brazilian law the guarantee was "void" because it was not authorized by the guarantor's board of directors. New York law does not contain that requirement. Of course, the guarantor argued that Brazilian law governed the question of whether the guarantee was a viable instrument. The plaintiff-beneficiary argued that New York law governed that issue. The Court of Appeals had to decide which law to apply to determine whether the guarantee was enforceable.

While the extension of the loan provided sufficient consideration under New York law to support the guarantee, the court's decision did not address

1. This chapter is based on and draws material from § 16X:15 ("Bad Law???; Bad Lawyering!!!") of *Commercial Agreements*, *supra*.

that issue. Instead, the Court simply held that "New York substantive law" governed and, accordingly, that the guarantee was enforceable. In arriving at this conclusion, the Court cited Section 5-1401 of the New York General Obligations Law allowing, as mentioned above, parties to a contract involving at least $250,000 to select New York law to govern their contract regardless of the relation to New York State.

15.2 The Lesson

Regardless of whether you believe the Court's ruling was correct—and I don't[2]—allow me, as Mr. Jaggers (Charles Dickens' *Great Expectations*) would say, to "put a case". Assume that the winning plaintiff has to enforce the guarantee in Brazil because that is where all of the assets of the guarantor reside. Will the Brazilian courts honor the New York ruling or will they find, instead, that enforcing an instrument "void" under Brazilian law to be against public policy, and, therefore, deny collection? Anyone want to take that risk?

In my own practice, I had a comparable situation.

Some years ago, "when I wore a younger man's clothes",[3] I was correspondent counsel in New York to a major British law firm. A client of that firm, an English company, was about to license some of its intellectual property to a Japanese company for use in Japan. The parties had agreed that the law of New York, a neutral jurisdiction, should govern the license under previously mentioned Section 5-1401 of the New York General Obligations Law. So the British firm asked me to prepare the license. "OK," I said, "but equally important as the contract itself is what the law is in Japan to protect the intellectual property. We must retain counsel in Japan."

---

2. I believe the court erred in refusing to apply the substantive law of Brazil to the validity of the guarantee, because the validity of an instrument in its creation — in its conception — should be a matter of local law governing the authority of the issuing entity to issue that instrument. I find no difference — at least no material difference — between (A) whether an entity has been properly constituted under the law of the jurisdiction in which it is organized (clearly a matter of local law), and (B) whether an instrument has been properly constituted under the law governing the authority of the entity to create that instrument. For example, Section 505 of the New York Business Corporation Law requires, with certain exceptions, that the board of directors of a corporation fix the consideration, terms and conditions of any option to acquire shares of that corporation. As far as I'm concerned, regardless of the choice of law stated in the option agreement itself, it is "the given in geometry" that an option issued in violation of that requirement is void and, therefore, unenforceable.

3. From "Piano Man", by Billy Joel.

"Ahhh, you're right, Peter," replied my British counterpart. And we did; and all turned out well.

So, regardless of what law governs the contract, if the transaction involves a foreign jurisdiction (state or country), or involves a party located in a foreign jurisdiction, where you or your law firm does not practice, you *must* engage local counsel. Apart from the fact that not doing so is malfeasance, the cost of local counsel is an insurance premium; and that cost will surely be far less than the cost of litigation!

Chapter 16

Opinion Letters

Opinion letters are required in a variety of transactions. Invariably they are required from counsel to the borrower in lending transactions and from counsel to the parties in the acquisition of a business. Though my firm was often asked to give and gave opinion letters, I do not recall requiring an opinion from counsel to the other party. Why? Let's see.

A legal opinion deals—or at least it should deal—*only* with matters of law, and, as such, any attorney can render that opinion. Apart from a few easily and objectively verifiable items mentioned below, the opinion letter should *never* deal with facts, such as the warranties of the client—though, on occasion, I have seen lenders ask counsel for the borrower to opine as to certain of the borrower's warranties such as litigation and contracts to which the borrower is party.

An additional, crucial caution—one highlighted by the preceding chapter dealing with multi-jurisdictional transactions—is the necessity to retain local or special counsel whenever the transaction or an agreement involves either a jurisdiction in which the attorney issuing the opinion is not qualified to practice or an area of the law in which the attorney issuing the opinion lacks expertise.

The basic issues that opinion letters address are

1. valid existence and good standing of the entity, which are verified by "certificates of good standing" issued by the appropriate governmental agency;
2. authority of the entity to enter into and perform the agreement, which is verified by examining applicable law and the applicable corporate documents such as the certificate of incorporation and bylaws or the applicable LLC or partnership agreements;
3. proper authorization and execution of the agreement, which are verified by certificates issued by an appropriate officer of the entity

(A) attesting to enabling resolutions adopted by the directors, shareholders, or other applicable governing body or bodies, and (B) identifying those persons authorized to sign and their signatures;

4. compliance with applicable law;
5. whether any governmental approvals are required in connection with the enforceability of the agreement and, if so, whether they have been obtained;
6. enforceability of the agreement against the entity;
7. in the case of a financing transaction, the perfection of any security interests.

Of the matters listed above, the most important are items 6 and 7, enforceability of the agreement and, in the case of a collateralized loan, perfection of the security interests. Item 6 (enforceability) depends on items 1 through 5, and item 7 (perfection of security interests) is verifiable by the examination of and compliance with applicable law regarding the security interests involved. As to the critical issues, enforceability and perfection, *under no circumstance* should your client be expected to rely on the opinion of counsel to another party to the transaction.

* * *

Opinion letters are always seasoned with qualifications. In the case of enforceability, the opinion letter will contain a qualification for an event of bankruptcy and, when appropriate, a qualification as to limitations that a court of equity might impose as, for example, with regard to a remedy requiring specific performance.

Sometimes an agreement will require a party to cause certain things to happen for which that party might not have the necessary control. For example, an agreement might require a party to cause others to do certain things. In these cases the opinion should contain an appropriate qualification as to the possibility that the party might not have the control required to effect the desired result.

* * *

It is obvious that the attorney on either side of the transaction can issue an opinion as to all of the matters listed above. In fact, if I were the client, I would insist that my own attorney issue an opinion regardless of whether the attorney for the other party issues one. I think it is the obligation of the client's attorney to issue that opinion. As an example in point:

Long ago, "in a galaxy far, far away", I represented a European bank that was obtaining collateral to secure certain obligations owing to it. The party providing the collateral was not the debtor, and problems that could threaten the enforceability of the security arrangements existed because of the financial condition of the party pledging the collateral. At the initial meeting with the attorneys for the debtor and pledgor, the first words they said to me were, "Peter, we're only going to give you a qualified opinion." To which I replied: "I wasn't going to ask you for opinions. I'll give the bank my own." (I surely did not want on record qualified opinions from counsel to the other parties cataloging problems that they thought might arise with the security arrangements.)

As might be expected, the pledgor of the collateral declared bankruptcy. During the bankruptcy proceeding, my security agreement snared a tax refund in excess of one million dollars (a goodly some in that bygone era). The refund sailed right through the bankruptcy proceeding into my client's account and was applied, without opposition, to the debt it secured.

* * *

In the final analysis, if a legal opinion is required in respect of "another" party to a transaction, that opinion should be given by counsel to the party for whose benefit the opinion is rendered. From the client's point of view, if an opinion is desired from counsel to the "other" party, that opinion should serve only as a supplemental opinion: It should not be relied upon by the client's counsel in rendering its own opinion. It is the obligation of counsel to do the "legal" due diligence for its client and not to allow its client to rely on the "legal" due diligence of another!

Resource Materials: Opinion Letters

The following materials supplement the teaching in this Chapter. They are available on Westlaw to law students and their teachers without charge if the law school has a plan with Westlaw that includes *Commercial Agreements, infra.*

Commercial Agreements—A Lawyer's Guide to Drafting and Negotiating, Thomson, Reuters

- Chapter 13: Opinion letters (generally)
- Chapter 2B: Loan agreements
- Chapter 16: Corporate authorizations

Related Assignments

Problems 24 and 30, *Exercises in Commercial Transactions*, Second edition, (Carolina Academic Press).

Chapter 17

Employment Agreements[1]

Of all the contracts that populate the commercial world, employment agreements are one of the most abundant. They address a wide variety of topics, and the treatment of each topic depends on the negotiation and the practices of the employer. Here is a list of topics most often addressed:

- Period of Employment
- Compensation
- Benefits such as health insurance and retirement programs
- Duties; Title
- Outside Activities
- Early Termination by the Employer or the Employee with and without cause
- Definition of Cause
- Severance (employee dismissed without cause or leaves because of employer's breach)
- Ownership of Work Product
- Protection of Trade Secrets and other Proprietary Information
- Restrictions on Competitive Activities
- Vacation/Sick Leave/Other Leave Rights
- Indemnity and Officer and Director Liability Insurance.

Of these topics the one that requires treatment in this text is the restriction on competitive activities following termination of employment. Often linked

1. This chapter draws on materials in an article by the author, "Non-Compete Clauses: A Reasoned Approach", that appeared in the February, 2018 issue of the New York State Bar Association *Journal*.

to this topic is the protection of trade secrets and other proprietary information. Employment agreements properly contain mandates prohibiting employees from using or disclosing trade secrets and other proprietary information of the employer (i) following their employment, and (ii) during their employment, for any purpose other than performing their services for the employer.

The restriction on competitive activities generally embraces the solicitation of employees and customers of the business following termination of employment, and engaging in activities competitive with the business of the former employer.

A prohibition against solicitation of employees is understandable and appropriate, as the departing employee learned of them only through the departing employee's time with the company. But this restriction should be limited to employees of the business at the time of termination, and it should have an expiration date.

A prohibition against solicitation of customers is also understandable and appropriate for the same reason: it relates to knowledge gained during employment. But, again, the restriction should be limited to customers of the business at the time of termination and should have an expiration date.

We now arrive at the most sensitive topic: the employee's competing with the business following termination of employment. These clauses, by law, must be reasonable; and in light of the employer's business and the employee's duties, they must be limited appropriately in terms of geographical area of the restriction, period of the restriction, and scope of the activities restricted.

Laws of those jurisdictions applicable to the employment must be examined.

Further, the Federal Trade Commission has issued a rule banning post employment non-compete clauses that prevent workers, following termination of their employment, from accepting work in the United States or that prevent them from operating a business in the United States.

The rule does not apply to non-compete clauses entered into as part of a *bona fide* sale of a business or to a non-compete clause entered into by person as part of a *bona fide* sale of that person's interest in a business.

And the rule does not exempt compliance with state laws.

As of this writing, the rule is being challenged in the courts by the U.S. Chamber of Commerce and others. The Federal District Court for the Northern District of Texas, in the case of Ryan v. Federal Trade Commission, set aside the rule, banning enforcement, stating that the FTC exceeded its authority in issuing it. On the other hand, the Federal District Court for the Eastern District of Pennsylvania, in the case of ATS Tree Services v. Federal Trade Commission, came to a different decision from the Texas Court.

Because challenges to the rule are pending in multiple jurisdictions, and because of the likelihood of appeals, it may be some time after this writing before we know the final fate of the rule. As a precaution, non-compete clauses should be qualified by limiting their application "to the maximum extent permitted by law".

To the extent that the rule does not apply, and in case the rule ultimately is invalidated or limited, please be judicious in restricting employment after termination. Post Employment Activities require careful consideration because they can affect a person's—and even a family's—livelihood. As mentioned above, the activities restricted and the period and geographical area of the restriction must be reasonable. But restricting employment following termination of employment may not always be appropriate and should be examined carefully.

I find that employers often overreach in the case of restricting an employee's right to work following termination of employment. An article in the Sunday, May 14, 2017, Business Section of *The New York Times*, "Losing the Right to a New Job", illustrates the point. The article quite properly decries the extension of non-compete provisions to middle-level employees.

In my own practice I have noticed an overly aggressive use of these "non-compete" clauses by employers and a lazy (or perhaps desperate) acceptance of them by employees: Too often the protection is not styled to fit the risk.

Recently I represented a doctor joining a medical practice. The employment agreement prevented the doctor from practicing medicine within a specified geographical area for a period of three years after termination of his employment. That draconian clause would have crippled the doctor's ability to earn a living following termination of his employment, which the employer had the unilateral right to terminate without cause on 60 days' notice. So we pointed out to the employer that

(1) it gained no protection from that clause because the practice was subject to competition from other practices in the area, and there were numerous other doctors in our client's specialty whom those other practices could hire, plus

(2) the practice had the protection it needed by the clause preventing the employee from soliciting its patients.

The prospective employer agreed, and we worked out a solution that allowed our client to work for other practices in the area but precluded him from opening his own practice in that area for a specified period, which was entirely satisfactory to the client.

The solution also gave our client the right to terminate without cause on 60 days' notice.

These changes allowed the client to leave the practice after several months and obtain gainful, more satisfactory employment in the forbidden zone without harming the former employer. The separation was amicable.

On the other hand, a client, a holding company with subsidiaries in the oil and gas and transportation industries, hired a new CEO. The contract we prepared contained the basic protections discussed above: (1) an absolute prohibition from using and disclosing to others trade secrets and other proprietary information of the parent and its subsidiaries, (2) a prohibition from soliciting employees of the parent and its subsidiaries, and (3) a prohibition from soliciting customers of the parent and its subsidiaries.

Given the industries involved and the nature of the client's business, we saw no reason, following termination of the executive's employment, to restrict his employment with other companies.

* * *

The article in the *Times* emphasized the anti-competitive nature of the restriction on other employment. What concerns me more, though, is harm to the individual who may be precluded from earning a living. An executive, whom the *Times* article quoted, argued on behalf of employers that regardless of the level occupied by the employee, the restriction on working for competitors was an essential prophylactic because of the difficulty and expense involved in detecting violations of the confidentiality requirement and enforcing the provisions designed to protect the company's trade secrets. But there is limited logic to this argument because the restriction on working elsewhere must, by law, be for a limited period only, so ultimately the company must rely on the unlimited protection against the use and disclosure of confidential information.

It is essential that the employer and prospective employee consider and examine these clauses in context to determine what is reasonably necessary and appropriate under the circumstances. Initially, it is incumbent upon the attorney for the employer and its client to engage in these considerations before writing, rather than robotically plugging a standard form into an agreement, hoping that the other party will accept it "as is".

As noted in Part I, there is no shame in writing a fair agreement.

* * *

Before concluding this exciting examination of non-compete clauses, there are some refinements to consider.

With regard to a prohibition on employment elsewhere, that prohibition should never apply if the employee leaves because of a material breach of the agreement by the employer or if the employee is terminated without "proper cause". These two exceptions, though, should not apply to the protections against solicitation of employees and customers, and they should never apply to the prohibition on the use and disclosure of trade secrets and other proprietary information.

Resource Materials: Employment Agreements

The following materials supplement the teaching in this Chapter. They are available on Westlaw to law students and their teachers without charge if the law school has a plan with Westlaw that includes *Commercial Agreements, infra.*

Commercial Agreements—A Lawyer's Guide to Drafting and Negotiating, Thomson Reuters.

- Chapter 6: Employment Contracts

Other service-type arrangements

- Chapter 6B: Consulting agreements
- Chapter 6BB: Agency agreements
- Chapter 6BBB: Service contracts
- Chapter 6BBBB: Executive search agreements
- Chapter 6D: Management agreements
- Chapter 7: Finders' agreements
- Chapter 7A: Agreements with investment bankers

Related Assignments

Problems 7, 16 and 29, *Exercises in Commercial Transactions*, second edition, Carolina Academic Press).

Chapter 18

Shareholder Arrangements

I have nothing against shareholder arrangements. I just don't like shareholder agreements. The principles discussed in this chapter, which address the corporate format, are also applicable to limited liability companies and can be adapted easily to that type of entity.

Shareholder agreements are often used in privately held, close corporations to deal with such matters as control, representation on the board of directors, and restrictions on the transfer of shares which include rights of first refusal on proposed transfers. However, I prefer not to use an agreement to treat these matters.

Instead, I prefer to deal with control, representation on the board, and transfer of shares in the company's constitution: its articles or certificate of incorporation. Placing the provisions in the company's constitution has two benefits: it reduces the risks inherent in a contract—especially those of breach; and it eliminates the need to make each new shareholder a party to the agreement.

The provisions that deal with the transfer of shares are basically the same as those you would find in a shareholders' agreement, which require each shareholder to give the company and the other shareholders the right to purchase its shares before those shares can be sold to someone else. It is essential that the right of first refusal be given to both the company and the shareholders lest the company lack the required surplus to purchase the shares. The company is given the first right, but if the company does not exercise its right, then the right passes to the shareholders, who may then purchase the shares in proportion to the shareholdings of those exercising the right.

I deal with control and representation on the board by using different classes of stock which have different voting rights and which can be—but do not have to be—equal in all other respects. For example, each class will be entitled to elect a certain number of directors assuring the shareholders of each class representation on the board. Veto rights at the board level are handled by requiring agreement by each class of directors. Similarly, veto rights at the shareholder level are handled by requiring agreement by each class of shareholders. Vacancies in directorships may be filled only by the class of shareholders that elected the director whose vacancy is to be filled.

In that same review of *Commercial Agreements* cited in Chapter 13, which appeared in the May 24, 1994 issue of the *New York Law Journal*, Mr. Beaumont observed:

> The author's treatment of restrictions on voting and transfer of shares in Chapter 8, "Shareholders' Agreements," is creative and useful.

Now I mentioned above that the different classes of stock "can be—but do not have to be—equal in all other respects." For example, all the shares of the different classes may be plain vanilla common stock with equal rights to cash and stock dividends and to distributions on liquidation. However, there are situations for which different priorities between classes may well be appropriate. Take, for example, a venture in which one party has an idea for a business and another party will provide the financing for the venture. In this type of arrangement, the party providing the financing will probably want priority as to dividends and as to distributions on liquidation. Of course, the money party could provide the funding in the form of debt bearing interest with a right to convert that debt to stock. But another solution, one that eliminates the burden of interest-bearing debt, could be a "sexy" preferred stock which participates *pari passu* with the common shares in the equity of the company but which

> (i) has priority over the common shares with respect to dividends and with respect to distributions on liquidation, and
>
> (ii) has class voting rights assuring representation on the board and veto rights at the director and shareholder levels as discussed above.

* * *

.... Well, I've been trying now for a while to come up with a clever, meaningful ending to this Chapter. But I haven't been able to, so I'll just refer you to the Resource Materials below, which I hope you find clever and worthwhile.

Resource Materials: Shareholder Agreements

The following materials supplement the teaching in this Chapter. They are available on Westlaw to law students and their teachers without charge if the law school has a plan with Westlaw that includes *Commercial Agreements, infra.*

> *Commercial Agreements—A Lawyer's Guide to Drafting and Negotiating*, Thomson Reuters.

- Chapter 8: Shareholder agreements (including rights of first refusal)
- Chapter 8A: A participating (sexy) preferred stock
- Chapter 8B: Preemptive rights

Related Assignments

Problems 9 and 17, *Exercises in Commercial Transactions*, Second edition, (Carolina Academic Press).

Chapter 18A

Minority Interests in Privately-Held Companies

18A.1 An Investor with a Minority Interest

A minority interest of an investor in a privately-held company without an exit plan is virtually worthless—that is, for example, an exit plan under which the holder of the minority interest has the option to sell its interest back to the company under specified circumstances such as the failure, within a specified period, to meet certain targets or to go public. Any such option should be accompanied by either (i) a guarantee by one or more of the company's shareholders, or (ii) by an alternate option to sell the interest to one or more of the shareholders of the company. The security provided by the guarantee or alternate option protects against a default by the company, especially in the case of the company's not having the required surplus to purchase the shares.

See Resource Materials below for options and various methods of valuation.

Also, consider some of the shareholder arrangements discussed in Chapter 18.

18A.2 An Employee with a Minority Interest

Sometimes a privately-held company will issue or sell to an employee an interest in the company or grant the employee an option to purchase an interest in the company. In cases such as these—especially when the employee purchases the interest—consideration should be given, as long as the company remains private, to granting the employee a right to sell the interest back to the company

(i) if the employee dies or becomes permanently disabled, or

(ii) if the employee is dismissed without cause or leaves because of a material breach by the employer.

On the other hand, if an employee is dismissed for cause or leaves without cause, or if the employee dies or becomes permanently disabled, the company, as long as its shares are not publicly traded, may wish to have the right to repurchase the employee's interest.

Determination of the purchase price for the shares might differ depending on the situation: dismissal for cause or leaving without cause; dismissal without cause or leaving because of an employer's beach; and death or permanent disability.

See Resource Materials below for options and various methods of valuation.

Resource Materials: Minority Interests

The following materials supplement the teaching in this Chapter. They are available on Westlaw to law students and their teachers without charge if the law school has a plan with Westlaw that includes *Commercial Agreements, infra.*

Commercial Agreements—A Lawyer's Guide to Drafting and Negotiating, Thomson Reuters.

- Chapter 12, §12:1: Options Generally
- Chapter 12, §12:2: Employee Option;
  Company's Buy-back Right;
  Employee's Put to the Company;
  Different Methods of Valuation
- Chapter 6, §6:4A: Definition of "Cause"
- Various Methods of Valuation:
  Book Value, §6:6
  Based on Earnings, §6A:3;
  Fair Market Value Determined by Directors, §6A:2

Related Assignments

Draft an option granting the employee the right to sell its shares to the company if the employee is dismissed without cause or if the employee leaves because of a material breach of the employment agreement by the employer.

Chapter 19

Acquisitions

"Acquisitions...," you mumble, "this is going to be long and grueling and difficult."

No, not really. We've already covered a good portion of the material. So, as Beethoven did at the beginning of the last movement of his Ninth Symphony, let's recap:

Chapter 13. Term Sheets. Never a letter of intent!

Chapter 14. Confidentiality Agreements. Never disclose any technology or any other proprietary or confidential information crucial to the business! Show what it does, not how to create it.

Chapter 11. Representations and Warranties; Due diligence:

- Due diligence trumps representations and warranties!
- If the seller receives anything but the entire purchase price in cash, the seller is also a buyer. An acceptable alternative to all cash is cash plus a negotiable promissory note for the balance of the purchase price secured by an irrevocable letter of credit issued by a prime bank.

Chapter 12. Indemnities: In addition to covering breaches, cover claims containing allegations that would constitute a breach.

Chapter 15. Multi-jurisdictional Transactions: The need for local counsel!

Chapter 16. Opinion Letters. Don't rely on the opinion letter of counsel for the other party! You should be able to give your client the opinion.

Chapter 17. Employment Agreements: Important for key personnel remaining with the business. Powerful non-compete and confidentiality clauses that bind the seller and the shareholders of the company being acquired are essential.

Chapter 18. Shareholder Arrangements: For purchases of a partial interest in a company. Lodge those arrangements in the certificate or articles of incorporation rather than in an agreement!

So, what's left? Well, a few things.

Apart from the due diligence (Right, I'm not going to stop emphasizing that function), there are preliminary considerations that are primarily the responsibilities of the lawyers and the accountants. Some of these are:

- Tax and Accounting considerations, which will bear on the method to accomplish the acquisition (discussed in the next paragraph);
- Anti-trust laws;
- Governmental approvals.

As noted in Chapter 11 dealing with warranties, acquisitions can be accomplished in three ways, each with its own risks:

1. purchase of the business and assets of the company to be acquired;
2. purchase of the stock of the company to be acquired;
3. merger of the acquiring company and the company to be acquired. In this type of acquisition, there is no seller: All the participants are both sellers and buyers!

A stock purchase and a merger present the same basic risk: the acquisition of a company with all of its liabilities, both known and *unknown*. Even audited financial statements are not a fail-safe solution, as evidenced by the Hewlett-Packard incident discussed in Chapter 11. And due diligence can be of limited value when dealing with *unknown* liabilities. So the warranties in respect of liabilities take on added importance, though not without reservation in the case of stock acquisitions and mergers as discussed in Chapter 11.

On the other hand, the purchase of the business and assets of a company virtually eliminates the risk posed by unknown liabilities because in that type of transaction the buyer assumes only identified liabilities. One liability risk, though, that an asset acquisition does not eliminate, and one which even thorough due diligence might not detect, is a hidden or latent defect in an asset that is being purchased such as a flaw in machinery or software, or in inventory that is purchased for resale. The buyer should investigate the availability, cost and coverages of latent defect insurance to mitigate or hedge against that risk.

However asset acquisitions present their own set of problems:

- The transfer of assets and contracts can be a large, complicated undertaking, especially when intellectual property is involved.
- Sales and transfer taxes must be considered.
- Bulk sales laws must be consulted, and though the bulk sales law under the Uniform Commercial Code has been repealed in most states, there are bulk sales laws under state sales and use tax laws such as Section 1141 of Article 28 of the New York Tax Law.
- If the buyer acquires all the business and assets of a company—as opposed to acquiring just a division—the only remaining asset of the seller will be the proceeds from the purchase price, which probably will not remain in the company very long. So in these cases, the buyer should obtain a guarantee from the shareholders of the seller to secure the warranty and indemnity obligations as well as any other obligations that survive the closing. As an alternative or complement to a guarantee, consider escrowing a portion of the purchase price.

Though the examination of all contracts is critical in an asset deal to determine whether there are any prohibitions on transfer, they must also be examined in a stock deal and in a merger because some contracts may treat as a transfer a change in control or a merger regardless of the entity that survives.

Needless to say, regardless of the method by which the acquisition is accomplished, a thorough examination of all contracts is essential to ascertain (A) the extent of the target company's obligations under them, and (B) the contingencies or risks that could impact the company's rights under them.

* * *

As the foregoing reveals, an acquisition requires a team with expertise in many fields to deal with the many aspects of the transaction.

And with that background, I will commit your minds to the Resource Materials.

Resource Materials: Acquisitions

The following materials supplement the teaching in this Chapter. They are available on Westlaw to law students and their teachers without charge if the law school has a plan with Westlaw that includes *Commercial Agreements, infra.*

Commercial Agreements—A Lawyer's Guide to Drafting and Negotiating, Thomson Reuters.

- §16X:11: **Due Diligence**
- Chapter 11: Stock acquisition
- Chapter 15: Asset acquisition
- Chapter 3: Guarantees
- Chapter 2: Promissory notes
- Chapter 14: Letters of credit

Related Assignments

Problem 11, *Exercises in Commercial Transactions*, Second edition, (Carolina Academic Press).

Chapter 20

Options

I can't claim that options are among your basic agreements, but they are one of the most valuable of contracts.

An option is simply a right. In most cases it is either a right to purchase (sometimes referred to as a "call") or a right to sell (sometimes referred to as a "put"). Here we'll explore only the option to purchase, for in the transactional world (that is, the transactional world outside the realm of the securities industry), a right to purchase is the most prevalent of options.

Options to purchase come in two basic forms: (1) a straightforward option to purchase, and (2) a right of first refusal. The right of first refusal comes in two forms: (A) an option to buy based on the offer of a third party, and (B) an option to buy based on an offer of the owner.

The basic rule in writing an option is to **leave nothing to negotiation.** Exercise of the option must result, without further act, in the execution of a complete contract leaving nothing to be discussed or negotiated. Often I've seen contracts just give a party "a right of first refusal": nothing more, just "a right of first refusal to buy X"; and in the background I sense a litigator crouching like a spider waiting to pounce. And lest you think only an inexperienced attorney is capable of such a mistake, witness the allegations in a complaint filed in the New York State Supreme Court involving an option to purchase real estate in Manhattan. The option in question was written by two well-known New York law firms. The complaint stated:

> Pursuant to the Agreement, if [Plaintiff] exercised the option on or before January 31, 1995, then [Plaintiff] and [Defendant] were to enter into a definitive Contract of Sale of the Premises ... for the sum of $18,000,000 ... [with] a deposit in the sum of $1,800,000. The Agreement expressly provided that <u>the Contract of Sale was to be "reasonably satisfactory to [Plaintiff] and its counsel."</u> (emphasis supplied)

> Prior to January 1, 1995, [Plaintiff] attempted to exercise the option under the Agreement and advised defendant that it was ready, willing and able to enter into a contract of sale and make the required deposit.
>
> [Defendant], in response to [Plaintiff's] exercise of its option, proposed a contract of sale that contained terms that were not reasonably satisfactory to [Plaintiff] and its counsel. Among other things, [Defendant's] proposed contract (i) would have required ... (emphasis supplied)

..., and straight on 'til morning.

Apart from containing the entire contract of sale, the option agreement should have specified that exercise of the option would constitute execution of the contract of sale. It should also have required that the notice of exercise be accompanied by the down payment.

Again, no term should be left open. So, if at the time an option is granted the parties cannot determine or agree on what the price for the property should be at some time in the future, then the option agreement must contain a procedure to determine that price objectively, as for example, by appraisal or by formula.

* * *

An option addresses a transaction that *might* occur sometime in the future, so the attorney must, with the client, anticipate all aspects of that possible, future transaction and deal with all of those aspects in the option agreement as if the subject of the option were a transaction about to take place.

Thus, for example, if the option is to buy equipment, the option must contain the entire contract to purchase that equipment: specifications for the equipment, delivery terms, price, payment terms, warranties, and every other term of the purchase all the way to governing law. If the contract includes deferred payment terms with the seller's taking a security interest in the equipment, then the entire text of the security agreement must be included as an exhibit to the option agreement. And if the buyer is to issue its promissory note to evidence the debt and the payment terms, that note must also be added as an exhibit to the option agreement. Further, if a down payment is required, the down payment should accompany exercise of the option, and exercise of the option should constitute execution of all the agreements.

If any blank spaces, such as dates, must be completed when the option is exercised, the option agreement must specify how to complete those blank spaces. Their completion must be purely mechanical. For example, the date of the agreement should be the date the option is exercised. **Nothing must be left to discussion!**

The same rules apply to an option to lease: the entire lease agreement must be attached as an exhibit to the option agreement, with any blank spaces to be completed mechanically as specified in the option agreement. Further, the first month's rent and any security deposit should accompany exercise of the option, and exercise of the option should constitute execution of the lease.

* * *

Just a few more points before I release you.

I generally urge clients against granting rights of first refusal because the procedures involved are complex and take time to execute—a condition that can easily result in the loss of a buyer or loss of a market for the property. The sample rights of first refusal contained in the Resource Materials listed below will eliminate any doubt you may have. One exception, though, would be a closely held company where the shareholders of a corporation or the members of a limited liability company want to maintain control of the shareholders and members with whom they must deal.

If and when you do venture into a right of first refusal based on an offer by a third party, the option agreement *must* require the third party offer to be an all cash offer in a specified currency (*e.g.*, U.S. dollars) payable on closing of the sale. Lacking that requirement, the third party offer might contain terms that the option holder cannot match or may not wish to match, like a specific Picasso painting or an island in the Caribbean in exchange for the property subject to the option.

* * *

Yeah, options ain't easy. Luckily, though, this fossil had a career long enough to figure out many of them, which he has included in the Resource Materials that follow.

Resource Materials: Options

The following materials supplement the teaching in this Chapter. They are available on Westlaw to law students and their teachers without charge if the law school has a plan with Westlaw that includes *Commercial Agreements, infra.*

Mr. Siviglia will be happy to furnish teachers with materials not yet published. Teachers may contact him at psiviglia@aol.com.

> *Commercial Agreements—A Lawyer's Guide to Drafting and Negotiating*, Thomson Reuters.
>
> Mr. Siviglia will be happy to furnish teachers with materials not yet published. Teachers may contact him at psiviglia@aol.com.
>
> - Chapter 8: Shareholders' agreements including rights of first refusal
> - Chapter 8B: Preemptive rights
> - Chapter 12: Stock options and options to buy real estate, plus a batch more that I recommend as alternatives to sleeping pills
> - Chapter 15F: Option to purchase capital equipment (scheduled to be added by the 2027 Supplement)

Chapter 21

A Bit about Insurance

Although maintaining proper insurance protection is primarily the client's responsibility, in order to represent their clients well, transactional attorneys should have some knowledge of insurance, perhaps the oldest of hedges. So here we go.

Insurance, as you well know, protects against risks. The most common insurances are (1) property insurance, which protects against the risk of damage to and destruction of property, and (2) liability insurance, which protects the insured against the risk of claims by others because of acts or omissions by the insured. Automobile insurance and homeowner's insurance include coverage protecting against both of those risks.

In the transactional world, the insurance that most concerns attorneys is liability insurance; and the first thing that attorneys should know about liability insurance is that there are two kinds: occurrence based and claims made.

> Occurrence based insurance protects against incidents that occur during the policy period regardless of when the claim is asserted, whether it is asserted during the policy period or after the policy period has expired. Even though protection extends beyond the policy period, in certain situations, like the sale of goods manufactured under a license, it is advisable to extend the policy period beyond the date of the last sale in order to protect against claims based on an incident occurring at a later date as, for example, because of a latent defect. In cases such as these, the policy period should extend at least through any warranty period.

> Claims made insurance protects only against claims asserted during the policy period. It does not protect against a claim made after the policy period expires even if the cause of action arose during the policy

period. So with claims made insurance, it is essential to continue the insurance coverage after the policy period would have otherwise expired for at least the period of the applicable statute of limitations and, as an added precaution, for a bit more.

Also in dealing with claims-made policies, especially when purchasing new insurance or changing insurers, the insurer will want to limit or exclude coverage for claims made during the policy period that arose because of incidents that occurred before the inception date of the insurance. In these cases it is essential to purchase coverage for claims that may have arisen during a specified period prior to the inception of the coverage.

* * *

For some types of transactions, the contract will not only require one of the parties to maintain insurance, but it will also require the other party to be covered by that very same insurance as an additional "<u>named insured</u>". Examples are (1) a secured loan where the lender will be a "named insured" on the policy for the property serving as collateral, with the insurance proceeds payable to the lender except, perhaps, for minor damage, and (2) real estate construction contracts where the developer will be a "named insured" on the contractor's insurance policies.

In these cases, where a party is added as an <u>additional named insured</u> to the coverage maintained by another—and especially in the case of construction projects—I will urge my client to maintain its own backup coverage lest for some reason, as, for example, a breach of warranty, the insurance of the other party fails. The underlying insurance should reduce the cost to the client of its backup policy. Lenders will secure similar protection, requiring borrowers to purchase <u>mortgagee interest insurance</u>, which protects the lender against the risk of the borrower's coverage failing.

Insurance clauses in the contract will also require that the additional insured not be liable for premiums and that none of the insureds be co-insurers, bearing a portion of the burden for the risks covered. Insurance clauses will also limit deductibles and contain other requirements, all of which are treated in the Resource Materials cited below.

In the case of real estate developments, I insist that the developer purchase its own insurance and not rely only on being a named insured under the contractor's policy.

* * *

In another area, employment arrangements involve several types of insurance: health care and life insurance; officers and directors liability insurance; key man insurance.

Officers and directors liability insurance protects those individuals against liability for their acts and omissions. Generally, small, privately held companies will not incur this expense.

Key man insurance provides compensation to a company if a person crucial to its business dies or suffers a disability preventing the person from doing his or her job. This type of insurance is purchased only in rare situations.

Most businesses will offer their employees insurance programs covering one or more aspects of health care: medical, hospital, prescription drug, dental, and eye care, as well as life insurance. Depending on the success of the business, the company may change these programs from time to time. It is, therefore, vital that any employment arrangement allow the company to change its program without breaching its agreement with the employee.

* * *

Please don't forget contractual liability insurance to support indemnity obligations, discussed in Chapter 12.

And finally, three additional items to keep in mind:

(1) like indemnities, insurance is only as good as the credit worthiness of the insurer and the terms of the coverage;

(2) someone knowledgeable in the type of insurance with which you are working, must examine carefully the insurance requirements of the contract and the policy provisions; and

(3) in cases of significant property damage, retain an insurance adjuster as insurance against the insurance company.

Resource Materials: Insurance (including model insurance clauses)

The following materials supplement the teaching in this Chapter. They are available on Westlaw to law students and their teachers without charge if the law school has a plan with Westlaw that includes *Commercial Agreements, infra.*

Commercial Agreements—A Lawyer's Guide to Drafting and Negotiating, Thomson Reuters.

Mr. Siviglia will be happy to furnish teachers with materials not yet published. Teachers may contact him at psiviglia@aol.com.

- Chapter 5: Secured transactions
- Chapter 6: Employment agreements
- Chapters 6E, 6F and 6G dealing with Real Estate Construction Contracts
- Chapter 10: License agreements
- Chapter 11: Key man insurance (note 12)
- Chapter 15C: Equipment leases (contractual liability)

THE RIVER

(*A respite from Part II*)

Waters glide:
sleeping glass to the sky.

They tumble, twist—
effervescent
between the rocks,

and plunge,
scraping backs on granite,
flaring mist into the dawn.
The great fish rises,
and fooled,
explodes into the naked light
where,
after pounding minutes,
an agéd man
cradles the silver life;

but reflecting…,
lets his moment slip,
then flash beneath the moist mirror.…

The river runs
as it has and will
through his lease on time,
for here he returns always
to seek peace from the rapids
pounding in his mind.

Part III

Negotiating

Chapter 22

Overlawyering, or How to Lose a Deal

The essay that follows is reprinted here with the permission of Thomson Reuters. Apart for some minor changes, it is Chapter 18 of Siviglia, *Commercial Agreements, supra.* Notwithstanding the essay's title, "Overlawyering ...", I think our competing buyer for the premises, if that buyer actually understood the nature of the situation and what its lawyer was doing, was as much to blame as the lawyer.

There is one comment I would like to make, and this essay illustrates that point.

Frequently, people in conversation say to me "I need a tough, aggressive lawyer." I always reply: "A lawyer can only be as tough and aggressive as the situation allows. What you want is a smart lawyer." And what you hope for on the other side of the table is the smartest person on the planet. For unlike litigation, as emphasized throughout this work, the negotiation of a contract that embodies a business deal is not—well, at least it should not be—a confrontational event. It is an undertaking to build a consensus that benefits all parties, an undertaking that requires understanding and creativity

* * *

A fundamental requisite to negotiating effectively is knowing what is important. The corollary to this principle is knowing when to concede a point. Knowing when to concede can be just as important as knowing when not to: "yielding" is not "losing" when the person making the concession is not hurt or when the risk involved is minimal and can be contained. The art is to develop a plan to accommodate the concerns of both parties within the given circumstances. When done properly, it is more a joint effort than an adversarial proceeding.

Overnegotiating or overlawyering, on the other hand, is a cancerous aberration of the basic principle (knowing what is important) and its corollary (knowing when to concede); and the defective gene is carried by negotiators and lawyers who are pigheaded or inexperienced, or who just lack good judgment. Following is an example.

Some years ago a client called from London to tell me that he was interested in purchasing a building site in mid-town Manhattan. The site was unusually large—three-quarters of an acre—and was improved by a warehouse facility, which our client would demolish to build a high-rise luxury condominium. The broker had told our client that the premises were vacant but that the sellers had already agreed on a price with a major New York developer, and they were in the midst of negotiating a contract. Our client gave me the name of the sellers' attorney and the price our client would pay, which we later learned was only slightly more than what the other developer was willing to pay. I called the attorney.

It turned out that the premises were not *exactly* vacant. They were occupied by over 300 tenants who leased space to store files, records and other documents. The attorney explained that although the price had been agreed, the parties had been unable to reach agreement on the terms of the contract dealing with the tenants. Our price was acceptable, the attorney said, and if we could come up with a satisfactory solution to the tenant problem and close quickly, the site would be ours.

The danger, of course, that tenants pose to a developer is stifling the project. Before demolition and construction can begin, the developer must have vacant possession. A recalcitrant tenant can delay a project for years, causing substantial inconvenience and loss. A well-known incident illustrates the point. To construct the building where my office in Manhattan was located, 20 residential tenants and 10 commercial tenants had to be relocated in order to demolish the existing buildings. A total of $2.5 million was reportedly paid to some of the residential tenants to induce them to move. One lady, Jean Herman, refused to move, finally rejecting an offer by the developer of $800,000. The result: the developers had to leave her four-story rent-controlled brownstone standing and build around it. In her obituary, The New York Observer reported that her building "remains like a wart on the site of the sleek, grey stone office tower."

In our transaction, the tenant situation, according to the sellers' attorney, had killed several sales, including one to another high profile New York developer, who had been advised by his attorneys that it could take two years or more at a cost of millions of dollars to remove the tenants.

The first thing we did was review the leases to verify what the sellers' attorney had told us: all tenancies were for storage and expired within a few months or were terminable on 30 or 60 days notice. At the same time, we sent a team to the warehouse to check the entire premises to be certain that all of the space was used for storage and that no one was living there or using any of the space for business offices. Satisfied on both points, I then checked with landlord-tenant attorneys to obtain an estimate of how long it would take to remove any tenants who would not vacate their premises after their leases terminated. The estimate—because these were merely storage facilities and not living quarters or business offices—was a year or less.

Within two days after our client had first called about the opportunity, I called to apprise him of the situation: the leases were all terminable in a matter of months; it could take up to a year to remove tenants who refused to vacate their premises; and he should plan on spending about a million dollars to gain vacant possession. I also explained that since the premises were used only for storage, there should not be the same reluctance to move as if they were used for living quarters or business offices. In addition, I went on, we would have to hire a warehouse operator to manage the facility until the tenants were removed, and that person would eagerly pursue the tenants to relocate in his own facilities. "So," I said, "does the deal still look worthwhile pursuing?"

"Yes," came the reply, "go ahead."

We immediately called the attorney for the sellers and requested a contract. It would be the same, he said, as the one he was negotiating with the other buyer, containing the same provisions that had delayed their deal to the point of giving our client this opportunity. The law firm representing our competing buyer was one of the major firms in New York City with a reputation for being tough negotiators. They were living up to their reputation, driving the sellers' attorney—an able but ailing single practitioner on the edge of retirement—crazy. We were viewed as something of a "white knight".

When we received the contract, my real estate partner showed me the provisions over which the sellers' attorney had been agonizing. My partner said that he really did not know what to do. I read them.

Stated briefly (the provisions spanned six pages of double-spaced type), if the information furnished by the sellers about the tenancies was incorrect in any material respect, then the sellers were given an opportunity to cure the defect. If, however, the sellers failed to cure the defect, then they were given two choices: (A) pay the buyer's damages, or (B) pay the buyer's damages, refund the purchase price, and have the buyer reconvey the property to them. By the terms of the contract, buyer's damages were limited to actual out-of-pocket expenses paid as a result of the breach; yet the uncertainty of what this figure might be concerned the sellers; and the clause itself was an invitation to litigation. Also, the contract did not provide an outside date by which the buyer had to assert its claim. This omission not only heightened the sellers' uncertainty, but it kept open the door to damages that an outside date to assert a claim would have closed. In addition, the complexity of the provisions alone made the sellers nervous. Sometimes it is better not to give people choices: just keep it simple, plain vanilla.

From our conversations with the sellers' attorney, it was clear that he and his clients—an estate of which he was an executor and relatives of the decedent—were honest people. Mistake or oversight rather than intentional misrepresentation was the real risk. Yet we had reviewed the leases and had examined the premises and were satisfied that the risk was small. The logical question, of course, is why, if the risk was small, did the sellers not take it. Well, for one thing, they were not sophisticated real estate traders. In addition, their lawyer was extremely cautious, and both he and his clients had been intimidated by the attorneys for the other buyer. Finally, the seller that held by far the largest interest in the property was the estate; and the executors, who included the attorney for the sellers, feared that a loss would expose them to criticism by the heirs of the estate.

Thus, the opportunity existed; but to seize it, a move had to be made. I, therefore, rewrote the clause to provide simply that if the information proved false and, as a result, our client's ability to commence demolition of any building was materially impaired, and if the sellers failed to correct the defect, the transaction would be rescinded, the property would be returned to the sellers, and the purchase price returned to our client. In order to gain quick acceptance, we did not ask that the purchase price be escrowed until the required waiting period expired without a claim being made. We did not even ask that interest be paid on our money in the case of recision.

I then explained the proposal and the reasons to our client. He agreed. And so did the attorney for the sellers, reiterating that the clause in question had killed prior deals.

Within five business days from the date of the first phone call, we signed the contract. Thirty days later we closed title. During this period we hired a warehouseman to operate the facility and prepared all the notices required to terminate the leases. We sent these notices as soon as we took possession. Other warehouses flocked to the opportunity like sharks in a feeding frenzy. Tenants who advised they could not vacate within the required period were given whatever time they needed. No threats were made. No payment was made to induce any tenant to leave. No litigation was commenced. Within three and a half months the premises were vacated at a cost of about 5% of the original estimate. Demolition began shortly thereafter.

* * *

The other buyer and its attorneys either misread the risk or sought protections beyond what the risk warranted. As all of the tenancies were solely for storage, there was little, if any, likelihood of a holdover that would frustrate the development. The end result proved the accuracy of this conclusion. Thus, there was no need to insist on damages. If any information furnished about the tenancies was incorrect, the defect would be discovered quickly. So there was every reason to accommodate the sellers and specify an outside date by which the buyer would have to assert a claim. Persistence on these two peripheral issues and the complexity of the provisions that resulted from overnegotiating and overlawyering caused the sellers' hesitancy, which gave our client the opportunity to acquire the site.

The competing provisions of the other buyer and our provisions follow in the Appendix. The reader should note the following points in those of our competing buyer. Inconceivably, the provisions do not specify which party would pay the transfer taxes in the event the buyer rescinded the sale because of a breach and transferred the property back to the sellers. These taxes would amount to hundreds of thousands of dollars. The party conveying title [here the buyer] is primarily liable for the transfer taxes; but in this case the sellers, who would have made the mistake and who would be receiving back title to the property, should pay them. The transfer taxes alone were probably more than any damages the buyer would have incurred.

Moreover, key notice provisions are poorly drafted. Section 42(a) permits the sellers to cure a breach within the 120-day period specified in Section 41(b), yet Section 41(b) does not specify any 120-day period. It does specify a 60-day period measured from the effective date of a "cure notice", but Section 42(a) does not operate on the basis of a "cure notice". Section 42(a) also permits the buyer to give notice of a breach within the period specified in Section 41(b). Again, Section 41(b) specifies no such period, though Section 41(a) does. Although it would be possible to work through the provisions to arrive at a solution as one might work through a maze, the solution would not be free from doubt. In addition, the passage underscored in Section 41(a) was not part of the typewritten version but was added at a later date by handwritten insert. It is axiomatic that the greater the complexity, the greater the likelihood of oversights and inconsistencies such as these.

In the end, our simple provisions prevailed—one-third the length of those of the competing buyer, without provision for damages, with an outside date by which a claim had to be made, and specifying that the sellers would pay the transfer taxes in the event of rescission. The sellers and their attorney readily accepted these provisions because they reflected the reality and logic of the situation.

Appendix

I. Provisions drafted by competing buyer. The first section below, 41, deals with discovery of a breach prior to closing of title. It is included because essential references to it are made in the following section, 42, which is the point of concern.

41. (a) In the event of any material breach or misrepresentation in or relating to any of the covenants, facts, statements and information furnished or made by the Sellers in Paragraph "40" of this contract and or on Schedule "A" hereof, Purchaser may cancel this contract <u>provided that Purchaser gives notice to Sellers (in the manner provided in Par. 35) within five business days of the discovery by Purchaser of such breach or misrepresentation, or sooner if the closing date shall fall within such 5-day period in which case the notice must be given on or before the closing date</u>, in which case Purchaser will be entitled to the return of the Down-Payment, all interest earned thereon, and any actual out-of-pocket expenses, if any, paid by the Purchaser as the result of any such breach or misrepresentation, and it is distinctly understood that the Purchaser shall not be entitled to recover for any loss of opportunity, loss of income, loss of profits or diminution in value resulting from any such breach or misrepresentation. In the event of such a breach or misrepresentation, Purchaser may also elect to close title, in which case Purchaser shall not be entitled to any adjournment of the closing date or any damages on account of such misrepresentation or breach. If Purchaser elects to close title as referred to in the preceding sentence, Purchaser's above right to cancel shall be and become null and void.

(b) However, and anything hereinbefore contained to the contrary notwithstanding, if the Purchaser shall give the Sellers notice of cancellation as provided in Paragraph 41 (a) the Sellers shall have the right to give the Purchaser notice of their intent to cure such breach or misrepresentation (the "cure notice"), which notice must be given within five business days after the date of Purchaser's giving of notice of cancellation. If the Sellers shall give the said "cure notice" and shall cure such breach or misrepresentation within sixty days after the effective date of the "cure notice", then the Sellers' notice of cancellation pursuant to Paragraph 41 (a) shall be null and void and the closing will be adjourned until ten days after such cure has been effected and the Purchaser has received notice thereof. Time shall be of the essence as to the Sellers' right to cure and the Purchaser shall be entitled to all interest earned on the Down-Payment during the period of such postponement.

42. (a) In the event any material breach or misrepresentation relating to any of the facts, statements and information furnished and made by the Sellers in Paragraph 40 of this contract, and/or on Schedule "A" hereof, and if the Purchaser shall give written notice to the Sellers of the misstatement, inaccuracy, act or omission constituting such breach or misrepresentation, within the time and in the manner specified in Subparagraph "(b)" of Paragraph 41 and if the Sellers then fail to cure the said breach or misrepresentation within the period of 120 days specified in the said Subparagraph "(b)" of Paragraph 41 hereof, there shall, nevertheless, and notwithstanding the provisions of Paragraph 41, be no liability on the part of the Sellers for such breach or misrepresentation unless the Purchaser shall transmit to the Sellers, in the manner specified in Paragraph 35 hereof, a written "Claim For Indemnification", signed by the Purchaser, consisting of a request by the Purchaser that the Sellers indemnify it by payment to it of the actual out-of-pocket expenses paid by the Purchaser as the result of any such breach or misrepresentation by the Sellers relating to any of the facts, statements and information furnished or made by the Sellers in Paragraph 40 of this contract and/or on Schedule "A" and stating the amount of the said expenses with a detailing of said expenses.

(b) After the Purchaser has transmitted to the Sellers a "Claim For Indemnification" in the manner stated in the preceding Subparagraph "(a)" of this Paragraph 42, the Sellers shall have the right and the obligation to make payment to the Purchaser of either the amount provided for in "Payment Plan A" or "Payment Plan B", both described below, depending on which of the said two plans the Sellers shall then elect; it being understood and agreed that the Sellers shall have the right, in their sole and absolute discretion, to decide and determine which of the said two plans for payment they shall elect:

> "Payment Plan A". The Sellers may elect to pay the Purchaser the indemnity that is provided for in Subparagraph "(a)" of Paragraph 41 of this contract pursuant to and subject to the provisions and limitations set forth in the said Subparagraph "(a)" of Paragraph 41.
>
> "Payment Plan B". The Sellers may elect to pay the Purchaser the same amount that is payable under "Payment Plan A" above, and, in addition thereto, the Sellers shall also have the right to rescind the sale and transfer of title that has then been made pursuant to this contract and to re-pay to the Purchaser the purchase price that was paid by the Purchaser to the Sellers pursuant to this contract and, simultaneously with making the said re-payment, to receive from the Purchaser a deed re-conveying to the Sellers the property that is the subject of this contract free from any liens or encumbrances on title other than those physical encroachments and covenants of record existing on the date of closing of title that took place pursuant to Paragraph 18 hereof.

(c) Within ninety (90) days of the mailing by the Purchaser to the Sellers, in the manner specified in Paragraph 35, of the "Claim For Indemnification" referred to in Subparagraph "(a)" of this Paragraph 42, the Sellers shall notify the Purchaser, in writing, likewise transmitted in the manner provided for in Paragraph 35 hereof, which of the above-described two payment plans the Sellers have elected—"Payment Plan A" or "Payment Plan B". The rights and obligations of the parties hereto with regard to the payment to be made by the Sellers to the Purchaser shall then be as specified in "Payment Plan A" or "Payment Plan B", depending on which of the said two payment plans has been elected in the aforementioned manner. If the Sellers shall fail to elect one of the said two payment plans in the manner and within the time above provided, "Payment Plan B" shall be deemed to have been elected and shall be applicable.

(d) The amount claimed by the Purchaser, as set forth in any "Claim For Indemnification" transmitted by it to the Sellers pursuant to Subparagraph "(a)" of this Paragraph 42 shall be deemed to be solely a statement by the Purchaser of the amount claimed by it.

The amount and the facts asserted in any such "Claim For Indemnification" shall not be binding on the Sellers nor presumptive and shall be regarded solely as the assertions of the Purchaser in support of such claim. However, in no event shall the liability, if any, of the Sellers as set forth in Paragraph 41, Subparagraph "(a)", exceed the amount stated in the said "Claim For Indemnification", if any, of the Purchaser or the amount provided for in Paragraph 41, Subparagraph "(a)", whichever is less.

(e) In the event that "Payment Plan B" described in Subparagraph "(b)" of this Paragraph 42 is elected by the Sellers, the closing of title in connection with the re-conveyance to the Sellers of the property that is the subject of this contract shall be held at 11:30 o'clock, A.M., ninety (90) days following the date of the mailing by the Sellers of their Notice of Election of "Payment Plan B" pursuant to Subparagraph "(c)" of this Paragraph 42, or, if said ninetieth day is a Saturday, Sunday or national holiday, then on the next succeeding business day, at the office of the attorney for the Sellers. Payment of any indemnity owing from the Sellers to the Purchaser pursuant to Paragraph 41, Subparagraph "(a)", of this contract shall likewise be made on the said ninetieth day following the mailing of the Sellers' notice of election of either "Payment Plan A" or "Payment Plan B", whichever is elected by the Sellers or on the next succeeding business day if same is a Saturday, Sunday or national holiday.

(f) In order to preserve the right of the Sellers to elect "Payment Plan B" referred to in Subparagraph "(b)" of this Paragraph 42 and thereby to rescind this sale and the conveyance made pursuant to this contract and to receive back the land and the buildings situated thereon that are the subject of this contract, it is understood and agreed that if the said buildings or any one or more of them are demolished, and if the Purchaser failed to transmit to the Sellers, in the manner provided for in Paragraph 35 hereof, the "Claim For Indemnification: provided for in Subparagraph "(a)" of this Paragraph 42 at least ninety-five (95) days prior to the commencement of the demolition of whichever of the said buildings is demolished first, any and all rights of the Purchaser to make and transmit to the Sellers the aforementioned "Claim For Indemnification" shall terminate and cease and any and all rights of the Purchaser to receive or recover any sums from the Sellers for any breach or misrepresentation, if any, shall also terminate and cease.

II. Provision as redrafted for our client.

42. (a) In the event any material breach or misrepresentation relating to any of the covenants, facts, statements and information furnished and made by the Sellers in Paragraph 40 of this contract and/or on Schedule "A" hereof, and if the Purchaser shall give written notice to the Sellers of the misstatement, inaccuracy, act or omission constituting such breach or misrepresentation on or before January 31, 1989, and if the Sellers then fail to cure the said breach or misrepresentation within the period of 120 days after receipt of such notice, the sale and transfer of title that has then been made pursuant to this contract shall be rescinded and Sellers shall pay to the Purchaser the purchase price that was paid by the Purchaser to the Sellers pursuant to this contract including all interest earned on the deposit [made on signing the contract of sale] held in escrow and, simultaneously with making the said payment, the Sellers shall receive from the Purchaser a deed re-conveying to the Sellers the property that is the subject of this contract free from any liens or encumbrances on title other than those physical encroachments and matters of record existing on the date of closing of title that took place pursuant to Paragraph 18 hereof; and Sellers shall pay all costs (including transfer taxes) incurred in such reconveyance.

(b) The closing of title in connection with the re-conveyance to the Sellers of the property that is the subject of this contract shall be held at 11:30 o'clock, A.M., ten (10) days following the expiration of the aforesaid 120-day period. If such tenth day is a Saturday, Sunday or national holiday, then the closing shall be on the next succeeding business day. The closing will be held at the office of the attorney for the Sellers.

(c) The provisions of this Paragraph 42 for the rescission of the sale and the conveyance made pursuant to this contract and for payments provided for will terminate if and when Purchaser demolishes any of the buildings that are the subject of this contract.

(d) For purposes of Paragraphs 41 and 42, a breach or misrepresentation shall not be deemed to be material unless the effect of such a breach or the true fact(s) in the case of a misrepresentation shall result in material interference with Purchaser's ability to commence, prior to February 1, 1989, the demolition of any of the structures on the Premises.

Chapter 23

Four Basic Principles of Negotiating: "BLIP"

The essay that follows is reprinted here with the permission of Thomson Reuters. It is a slightly modified version of Chapter 19 of *Commercial Agreements, supra*, and there is some overlap with prior material; but, as my wife, the teacher, says, repetition is often good.

* * *

Overture: Should We Take a Course in How to Negotiate?

Some time ago, a neighbor of mine, a businessman, told me that he was taking a course in negotiating. The course had mock negotiating sessions, and my neighbor said, with smug confidence, that the one principle he had learned was that after the parties establish their positions, the person who opens his mouth first loses. That observation is true in such a limited number of situations that it would be misleading to raise it to the level of an axiom. Further, the idea of taking a course in negotiating strikes me as absurd, for *like sex, negotiating is not something you can learn from a book or in a classroom.*

A person learns to negotiate by negotiating. And the human being, of necessity, begins to learn the technique from childhood, seeking from the earliest ages to get what it wants by whining, squealing and screaming.

The pressure of time cannot be created in the classroom. The reality of negotiating cannot be simulated there. In a staged negotiation, nothing is at stake. No one is at risk; there are no financial consequences. An actual job does not hang in the balance. An acquisition, a financing, a contract for the construction of an $80 million ship does not depend on the outcome. The parties to the classroom negotiation leave the table as they arrived. Beyond the classroom, parties' leaving the table as they arrived can only happen when the negotiation fails. All participants maneuver to gain as much as possible without losing the deal. The desire for gain and the fear of losing an opportunity are the centripetal forces that keep the parties in orbit, that keep them searching for solutions. For example, when the publisher and I negotiated the contract to publish my first book, we quickly reached agreement on all but one of the points. On this one issue I could not accept what the publisher wanted, and what I proposed was unacceptable to the publisher. But the publisher wanted the book enough and I wanted that publisher to publish it enough to make us jostle and jostle until we fashioned a solution.

The desires and fears that drive the parties toward agreement cannot be engendered by simulation. They can only be experienced when an opportunity is at stake. Yet sometimes the differences on one or more fundamental issues are too great. In those situations, it is natural and best not to conclude an agreement. But it is essential that the parties be imaginative and flexible, so that if agreement is not reached, the failure is due to genuinely incompatible positions—and not to stubbornness or a lack of creativity.

Another reason mock negotiating sessions are deceptive caricatures is they cannot realistically duplicate an entire transaction. The acquisition of a company, a financing, the arrangements to form a business or joint venture, a contract to publish a book: all of these do not begin and end within a classroom period. Depending on size and complexity, they take days, weeks, and even months to conclude. And they are continuous, without scheduled breaks as there are between classes.

Just before writing this chapter, I closed a management buyout that tested the patience of the participants for over nine months. The situation was quite desperate for my client, the seller, because his wife was terminally ill, and unknown to me, so was he.

When management could not perform the terms originally agreed, a relatively simple transaction was renegotiated and became more complex. These new arrangements, though, raised problems with the company's bank that could not be resolved; so the management team had to change banks to conclude the deal. Now, points negotiated once and renegotiated had to be negotiated again; and the transaction became still more complex. Not unexpectedly, participants from time to time threatened to abandon the deal. But these gestures were merely feints from frustration to accelerate the process. As the transaction developed and evolved, the parties, as they often do, became more involved, more committed (like being drawn into a vortex) and were less likely to quit. With so much time and energy invested, the alternative—*i.e.*, not closing—usually becomes more distasteful. Now, at 5:00 p.m. on the day before the closing, the management team called to tell me of a last minute impasse with the new bank that would kill the deal. "Peter," they asked, "could you agree to a new arrangement that would solve the problem and save the deal?"

I said that I would have to think about any new arrangement, explaining that even if agreement could be reached, it would require changes in the documents, would delay the closing, and would make the lawyers even richer. "I'm going home," I said, declining an invitation to join the discussions, knowing that if I did join, my client would only lose. Experience had taught that the management team would have to accommodate the bank, because not closing at this stage would have been a disaster for the business and so for the futures of all concerned. The decision to decline the invitation was a tactical risk far less than the risk involved in accepting it.

My wife complained that I did not sleep well that night, flapping around like a flounder out of water. But when I returned to my office in the morning, I found a fax timed 12:48 a.m. (ah, yes, this was still before creation of the internet) confirming that the closing would take place as scheduled.

No classroom simulation can create these pressures or impart the knowledge necessary to deal with them effectively. No matter how powerful the intellect, no matter how many negotiating techniques it devours, without sufficient experience programmed into the data base, the individual will not possess the judgment required to assess a situation properly and to know with confidence what to do and when to do it. And a lack of confidence makes a person a weaker and less effective negotiator.

... Well, now that I have explained why it is useless to read further, I will continue.

* * *

The discipline of negotiating reminds me of a passage from "The Gambler", Kenny Rogers 1979 award-winning song, written by Don Schlitz:

You got to know when to hold 'em,
Know when to fold 'em,
Know when to walk away,
and know when to run.

Indeed! But the question remains: How do you know when to hold 'em, know when to fold 'em, know when to walk away, and know when to run? The answer, of course, is *experience.*

* * *

Four basic principles dominate the discipline of negotiating, and "**BLIP**" is the acronym identifying those four principles: **B**elief; **L**everage; **I**mportance; **P**atience.

* * *

B. Belief (Never Bluff)

You must make the other party to the negotiation believe that what you say you mean and that you are prepared to stand by that position even though you may lose the deal. Of course, this position must be taken only on issues of importance (a topic treated below). Never bluff. If you bluff and get caught, you lose credibility. And once credibility is lost, the other party will not take you seriously and will probably be able to push you further on other points than if you had not been caught in the bluff. The following incident provides a fine example, though, for a lawyer, it did amount to dancing on a narrow ledge.

Some time ago a client, and also a friend, called from overseas to brag to me that he had just done a wonderful deal. He explained that he and a competitor, a business colleague, were bidding against each other on a project. During the bidding process, they decided that it was silly for them to compete against each other, so one of them would withdraw. If the one who remained in the bidding process was awarded the project, then that person would compensate the other who withdrew. My friend withdrew.

"Wonderful," I said sarcastically. "If you did that in the United States, you would have violated the law and made an illegal and unenforceable contract. I hope you have something cleverly written assuring you of payment."

"He's my buddy," came the reply. "I don't need anything in writing."

"Don't bet on it," I said.

A few weeks later an agitated friend called to tell me that his "buddy", whom we'll call Bert, had won the bid but was refusing to honor the promise he had made.

"Start the meter running," my friend said.

I told him that I probably could get him paid but that he would have to do exactly what I told him to do and that he had to be prepared to discredit himself publicly. "I'll do anything," my friend said, furious at being stiffed.

I had my friend write a letter to Bert stating that if the "matter" (of course, without description) was not resolved within two weeks, he would either disclose the arrangement to the project owner or bring the issue for redress before Bert's Board of Directors. "You can't bluff," I said. "You better mean what you say and make him believe that you mean it."

"Don't worry, I will!" And my friend certainly did.

There was an immediate response. Ugly negotiations followed in which my friend, by his statements, tone and demeanor, made it clear to Bert that he was not bluffing and that he would not be cheated, even if he had to discredit both of them publicly.

During the negotiations, my friend called: "Peter," he said, "Bert asked me which course of action I would take if the matter is not resolved."

I told him to reply: "If you want to find out, call the hand," thereby heightening Bert's uncertainty and anxiety. Clearly Bert concluded that paying a substantial sum was preferable to the risk of losing a huge project as well as one's name, dignity and job.

Within two weeks the matter was resolved, and my friend received full payment: more than U.S.$400,000 in the foreign currency.

I didn't charge him. Engineering the enforcement of an unenforceable arrangement was sufficient compensation. And, after all, he was—and still is—my friend.

The corollary to Never Bluff is the art of detecting a bluff.

A client of mine, Michael, was advising a major, multinational company, which I'll refer to as the Buyer, on the purchase of a portion of the film library of a famous Producer. The Producer's warranties respecting the films were to be secured by collateral under a security agreement that the attorney for the Seller had written—a big **NO NO** if you're the creditor. Incredibly, the attorneys for the Buyer, a major International law firm, did not know how to deal with the agreement or with the Producer's nasty, tenacious attorney, who was actually bullying them. Michael suggested that the Buyer ask me to handle the security arrangements as I was—at least at that time—an expert on secured transactions.

The security agreement that the Producer's attorney had written was actually an **INSECURITY** agreement. So I wrote a proper agreement with which the Buyer and its attorneys were quite pleased. The Buyer was so anxious to close the deal that it wanted to have a meeting that very day with the Producer's lawyer and executive officer, and give them the new agreement at that meeting to review.

Now here I am gong to emphasize something you should never do. I told the Buyer's executive "**NO!** You never present a document at a meeting and ask the other party to read and comment on it at that meeting. It's not right. It's not fair."

So we had the agreement delivered to the Producer's lawyer and met with them the next day at my office.

Immediately the Producer's lawyer said he would not deal with the agreement I had written and demanded comments on his draft. I told him in no uncertain terms that his agreement was a farce, and we'd be working with mine. "I'm not putting up with this crap", came the lawyer's reply. "We're leaving." "OK", I said, "you know where the door is—Leave."

"No, Peter, NO!!!" yelled the Buyer's executive. "You're killing the deal." To which I replied in my finest "Brooklynese": "Shut up or get another lawyer". Michael, my client who had introduced me to the Buyer, motioned him to "cool it". He did, and the Producer's attorney and executive officer left.

"Just sit tight," I said. "They're bluffing. They're counting on you to run after them. They'll be back in ten minutes." Well, I was wrong. They were back in five, and agreed to sign what I had written without change.

How did I know they were bluffing? The Producer was selling a substantial part of his film library. Obviously he needed the money. His minions weren't going to blow the deal over a security agreement, because the Producer would have blown them away. The situation was easy to read.

Another example of detecting a bluff appears under the third letter of our acronym, "I".

Now before turning to the Second letter of our acronym, "**L**", let me give you a footnote to my statement about **NOT** presenting a document at a meeting for the other party to review at the meeting. The footnote is consistent with the letter "B": **BULLYING.**

Another client had arranged a syndicate of lenders to finance management's taking private a publicly-traded real estate company. At the opening of the first meeting, the company's attorney, a high profile real estate lawyer in New York, handed me an agreement, stating that he would like it signed that afternoon.

I immediately returned the agreement to him, saying that we weren't going to sign anything that day, and if we ever signed anything, I would write it. The CEO immediately shut down his attorney.

Not only should you never present a document at a meeting for the other party to review at that meeting, you should **never, never** let anyone do that to you.

* * *

L. Leverage (Understanding the Leverage)

You must know who has the leverage, know when it begins to shift, as it often does, and understand how to use it effectively when you have it. When money is involved, the human animal will generally act rationally, and knowing this, allows you to safely predict how it will react in given situations. But you must never push the other side to the point of irrationality because irrationality cannot be predicted and you, therefore, lose your advantage. Push 85 to 95%; never 100%.

Our firm obtained judgment for a substantial amount for a client. For some reason—irrelevant here—the lawyer in charge of the matter agreed not to enforce the judgment for a period of time. Nevertheless, that same lawyer attached the defendant's bank account, corralling a substantial sum; but he did not seek to enforce the attachment. He believed that the attachment alone did not violate the agreement not to enforce the judgement. The defendant's attorney thought—not without reason—to the contrary; but he was willing to negotiate. He proposed assigning to our client a charter party (a lease of a ship) to secure payment of the judgment in exchange for releasing the attachment. As I had expertise in this type of contract, the lawyer in charge of the matter at our firm came to me for advice.

I looked at the proposed collateral and determined that it was worthless because, in fact, no charter had been signed. Instead, the parties merely had an informal and unenforceable arrangement. I explained to the defendant's attorney why the proposed collateral was not satisfactory. Angry, the attorney threatened to sue for breach of contract, alleging that if the funds were not released, a payroll would be missed and the defendant, which was in precarious financial condition, would have to file for bankruptcy protection. The damages would be enormous, he cautioned.

Other attorneys in our firm who doubted the validity of the attachment, were becoming concerned. They wanted to call the client to get permission to release the attachment.

"No," I said. "The issue is not entirely free from doubt. These guys will cave—if not today, tomorrow; and if not tomorrow, then on the steps of the courthouse. No one will trade viability for bankruptcy and a lawsuit. They're not going to commit economic suicide. Just be patient."

The attorneys, though, decided to call the client; but—*miracle of miracles*—while they were actually on the phone with our client, the attorney for the defendant called me and said that the defendant would pay 50% now and 50% at a later date. I immediately interrupted the call with the client. Adequate arrangements were made to assure payment of the 50% balance, and I asked for interest at 18% per annum on that balance (short term rates were about that at the time). "Outrageous," cried the defendant's attorney, "you're holding us up."

"No," I said, "this is a market rate. We're not going to finance your obligation without charge."

The defendant and its attorney reluctantly agreed. Here I may have pushed more than 95%, but, given the circumstances, the result was not in doubt.

On the other hand, though, as important as it is to know when and how to use the leverage you have, it is just as important to know what to do when you don't have leverage. The topic that follows contains an example of that very situation when representing a borrower seeking a loan from a bank.

* * *

I. Importance (Knowing What Is Important)

Knowing what is *important* is crucial to the success of most negotiations.

To conduct a negotiation effectively and successfully, the parties must focus their efforts on the important issues, and generally there are only a few of these. For this reason, in any negotiation, I recite the Lawyer's Prayer:

Please, let the smartest person in the world be on the other side of the table.

I have never seen anyone gain an advantage negotiating against inexperience or ignorance. The inexperienced person tends to treat all points as having equal importance and has difficulty making decisions. The ignorant person will freeze on a point, lacking the understanding and flexibility to find or contribute to a solution. Good negotiators determine from the outset what issues are important to their side and what issues are important to the other side. They then try to obtain as much as they can of those that are crucial to them and try to accommodate the other side as much as possible.

One of our clients was building a condominium in New York City. It was important to have the concrete work done ahead of schedule. Two of the developers told me that the contractor would agree to complete the work by the specified date but wanted a bonus, specifying the amount. I asked whether the amount requested was satisfactory. They said "yes", so I suggested that we agree to the amount but insist that the work be completed by the required date without regard to *force majeure*, that is, regardless of strikes, weather and other events or circumstances that might delay performance. The contractor was happy that we accepted his figure but insisted on extending the completion date because of delays due to *force majeure.* We explained that if the work was not done by the required date, regardless of the reason, we would gain no benefit. That date was essential to us and that is why we accepted his figure, but we could not agree to *force majeure.* The contractor, though, refused to yield; and late one Friday afternoon, the principals called to tell me that the contractor threatened to walk off the job unless we agreed to the *force majeure* provision. At that time we owed the contractor a substantial sum. His walking off the job would be a breach of the contract, and he would be liable for damages. The contractor knew all this, so I told my client he was bluffing. "Peter," they said, "if you're wrong, we lose thousands of dollars a day!"

"I'm not wrong," I insisted. "He's bluffing." We argued for a long time, and eventually, reluctantly, they agreed to follow my advice. Again, my wife reminds me that I flapped around like a flounder that night. But at 10:30 Saturday morning, one of the developers called to tell me that the contractor was on the job with a full crew. We never did sign an agreement to accelerate the work. Nevertheless, the contractor completed the work by the date we had set, and we paid him the bonus he had requested.

Another incident in the same project produced a further example of how essential it is to identify and hold firm on issues important to your client's interest. ***No deal at all is always better than a bad deal.***

At the beginning of the project, one of the principals arranged a sale of several units to a Middle East group based in Kuwait. The price and units were agreed, but instead of the customary cash deposit, the down payment to secure performance of the contract was to be made by a letter of credit (essentially a bank guarantee of payment). When discussions on the contract began, the buyer insisted that the letter of credit be for 10% of the purchase price. I said we would accept no less than 20%, because at 10% the contract would be no more than an option, and a buyer would readily forfeit that amount to get out of the contract if the market dropped. We negotiated late into the evening on a sweaty summer night filled with their cigar smoke. I wouldn't budge; I wouldn't go to 15%; I wouldn't go to 18%; I wouldn't go to 19%. Finally the buyer agreed: 20%.

Later, when the building was completed, we gave our 30-day notice of closing. Within a few days, the buyer asked to extend the closing date: The Kuwait stock market had just crashed.

"Sure," I said, "just close on one of the units and we'll extend another 30 days on the rest."

"No, we want to extend on all," came the reply.

"Forget it," I said, "I'll draw the letter of credit if you don't close."

This they surely didn't want because they would have to reimburse the bank immediately for the amount we drew. They even got the lead developer who had arranged the sale to call me to instruct me not to draw the letter of credit.

"No way," I explained. "They're trying to get out of this contract. You've got two partners and a bank. They've got to buy at least some of the units!"

The exchange grew bitter. His two partners, who were in my office at the time, were listening silently, nervously to the call. But finally the lead developer relented. "All right, Peter, do what you want," he exclaimed angrily, and hung up.

As the end of the 30-day period neared, the buyer retained a major New York law firm to negotiate. Of course, their first thrust, after being convinced that we would not extend without consideration, was to threaten a lawsuit to stop us from drawing under the letter of credit.

"Look," I said, "you may enjoin us for a week or month or even two months, but you know and I know that eventually you'll lose and we will draw against that credit. Just close on some of the units and we can do a deal."

My client and the buyer continued negotiations, and finally, on day 29.5, the buyer purchased half the units, and we cancelled the balance of the contract and returned the letter of credit. During that same period we learned that many foreign buyers of units with 10% deposits in a competing New York condominium project had walked away from their contracts. Their currency had collapsed against the U.S. dollar, making the price they were to pay for their units in U.S. dollars unaffordable. That competing project was Trump Tower.

The corollary, of course, to focusing on the important is ignoring the unimportant. Often this is difficult to do because the lawyer, himself, or the client feels that the job is being slighted. But the lawyer's experience must prevail both on himself and the client to serve the client best. For example, when I represent a borrower, I will not conduct extensive negotiations on the loan documentation because the lender's attorney has all the leverage before the funds change hands. Thus, what can be gained after the borrower and lender agree on the essential terms[1] is usually too meaningless to justify the expense of an in-depth negotiation. Also keep in mind that for every hour the borrower's attorney negotiates, the client pays for two, because the borrower also pays the fees of the lender's counsel. A few extra days on a grace period, when the last person in the world who wants to call the loan is the bank, is just

1. Amount of the loan; interest rate; conditions to drawing the funds; payment terms; collateral; and perhaps some covenants.

not worth it. I, therefore, concentrate on making sure the essential terms are correctly stated and that the covenants and warranties are not overbearing and are consistent with the nature of the transaction. Generally, the lender and its attorney will appreciate this approach, and it will aid in obtaining concessions where appropriate. For example, a loan agreement to finance the acquisition of a parcel of real estate improved by buildings that were to be demolished, required, as a matter of course, that fire insurance be maintained. When I pointed out that the buildings were to be demolished, the lender readily removed this requirement, thereby eliminating a substantial expense. In that same transaction the loan documentation, again as a matter of course, required audited financial statements from the borrower. When I explained the expense involved and that the borrower was a single purpose corporation with this real estate project its only business, the lender agreed to omit the audited financial statements, reserving the right to require them, if it wished, at a later date—a perfectly satisfactory arrangement (especially since we were in no position to ask for anything more).

The principles of knowing what is important and ignoring what is unimportant have an interesting application to negotiations directed to settling a dispute. Each side has its own perception of why it is right and why the other side is wrong, and invariably during the discussions—especially when they get a bit tense—one and then both sides will try to argue the merits of their claims. These arguments, though, are at best unproductive, for neither side will concede that the other is right; and at worst they will rise to a pitch that will shatter the discussions.

The purpose of the discussions is not to litigate the case but to create a solution: *i.e.* to reach an agreement; to do a deal. The lawyer, therefore, must not join in the joust, but defuse the fray. Thus, whenever a party to a settlement discussion begins to argue its case—whether that party be my client or the other side—I immediately redirect the discussion to the purpose for which all have assembled: developing a mutually satisfactory solution. "We're not here to try the issues," I will say. "Each side knows its and the other's position, and neither is about to agree with the other. We're here because everyone apparently agrees that settlement is the more attractive alternative. Certainly, reaching an agreement is preferable to the uncertainty and the cost of litigation, where the only sure winners are the lawyers. Arguing the case is for the courtroom, not the conference room; so let's focus on trying to get an agreement."

Frequently, the good negotiator will employ the techniques of a good mediator; and in no arena are the qualities of a mediator more important than the conference room where the settlement discussions are in progress: Have the parties park their guns at the door; identify those concerns most important to each side; identify those objectives of each side that do not threaten the other side or that threaten the other side the least; locate patches of mutual interest (the broadest often being the desire to avoid or curtail litigation); build compromise and agreement from those non-threatening and least threatening objectives and patches of mutual interest.

* * *

P. Patience

"Sitability" is another word for this principle. A corollary is **G** + **I** = **L**, where **G** = greed, **I** = impatience, and **L** = a loser.

Patience is most important in what are called "chicken" negotiations. These are negotiations which usually involve only one issue, and that issue is usually price. Each party has an acceptable figure in mind and the trick is to get as close to your figure as you can. I hate this kind of negotiation because logical applications are of little, if any, help; and here my neighbor's observation regarding the first to speak comes to mind. But someone has to speak sometime, and I see neither advantage nor disadvantage in making the first offer. If you are the buyer, the offer will always be below what you are willing to pay; and if you are the seller, it will always be higher than what you are willing to accept. But once a party makes an offer in this type of negotiation, that party should not make another proposal (that is, negotiate against itself) until the other party makes a counter offer.

In the same condominium project mentioned above, the principals arranged the sale of a great many units to a single buyer (not the buyer from Kuwait discussed above). The negotiations, in which I did not participate, were long and difficult; but finally one of the principals told me that they had reached agreement on the units and the price. The next day the attorney for the buyer had a contract for the sale of the units on his desk. He called me that same day or the next and said that everything was fine except that instead of paying 100X for the units, his client wanted to pay 95X and, in addition, as a condition to completing the sale, his client, wanted us to sell three of the units for his client's account. I replied that the price of 100X was agreed and we were not going to discuss it further. As far as selling three of the units for his client, that was out of the question. We would sell them for ourselves.

After we hung up, I told the principals of the conversation. They said they agreed with me on the question of selling three units for the buyer, but they also said that 95X was acceptable and we should take it. I told them, "If you go to 95X, they will go to 93.5X, and if you accept that figure, they will go lower again. *Sometimes to get a deal, you have to be prepared to lose it.*" Again I prevailed.

We heard nothing the next day. Silence again on the second day. When one of the principals suggested that I call the lawyer for the buyer to find out what was going on, with a bow to my neighbor, I declined. We were sweating, but the other guys were sweating just as much. On the morning of the third day, one of the principals called. "I guess we lost the deal," he said; to which I replied, "Don't bet on it." That afternoon the lawyer for the buyer called and said the buyer agreed to 100X and withdrew the requirement for the sale of the units. We simply "out-patienced" them.

Encore

Though conducting a negotiation is often exciting and fun—albeit nerve-wracking—it is sometimes better for the lawyer to be the coach, or the script writer and director, rather than the principal player.

A client in the shipping business had chartered in (leased) several vessels when the market was high. While the charters were still in effect, the market dropped severely causing losses which threatened the life of the company. The client, therefore, was forced to renegotiate several of its charters, an occurrence not uncommon in the shipping industry. All but one owner was accommodating, and for that one owner, the client called to ask my advice.

It so happened that I had written portions of the charter for this vessel and also an agreement giving the client the option to purchase the vessel at the end of the charter. Under the terms of the charter, the owner was required to record the option just as a mortgage is recorded; but the owner had not done so and was thereby in default. The client, however, had not pressed the issue for a very long time, so the owner had a good argument that the requirement had been waived. Nevertheless, it was the only lever available.

I told the client that we could demand that the owner register the option, stating that if the owner failed to do so, we would terminate the charter. I also explained that for this ploy to work, we would have to be prepared to terminate the charter and go to arbitration if the option was not registered. We were fairly certain that the owner would refuse to register the option, in part because the owner would probably have to obtain approval from the bank that had a mortgage on the vessel. In addition, the owner was from a country where settlement rather than litigation is the norm, so we were reasonably confident that the owner would negotiate if it believed that we would terminate the charter.

The following possibilities thus existed: If the owner did register the option, the client would have obtained its original bargain and we would have to return to the drawing board. On the other hand, if we had to terminate the charter and arbitration ensued, the damages that would be assessed against the client if the owner won would approximate the client's loss on the vessel had the charter not been terminated. The only risks then were attorneys' fees and the cost of arbitration, which were negligible in comparison to the potential benefit to be gained.

The client agreed to the strategy and we began. For technical reasons, the initial demand to register the option was sent by our attorneys in the country where the owner was located. Thereafter the communications were between the owner and our client directly. I prepared the communications for our client, which were then sent from its office. We did not respond to any of the owner's arguments that we were wrong. Instead, we just pressed our demand that the option be registered as required, stating that if it was not registered, we would terminate the charter.

As expected, the owner refused to register the option, and we sent the notice terminating the charter. The owner, now convinced that we were not posturing, asked for a meeting in New York. The client called and said that the owner wanted its lawyer present, and asked how he should reply. I told him to tell the owner: "If the lawyers must be present, don't bother coming because we will not attend." I knew the client would negotiate a better deal without the lawyers present. I wanted the parties to focus on amending the charter rather than discussing the merits of each party's position, an issue which the owner's attorney would surely raise and press.

The owner agreed to meet without attorneys. The client negotiated an excellent deal. I prepared an amendment to the charter, and I appeared only to discuss a few minor points in the amendment with the owner's attorney. After the amendment was signed, an appreciative client called: "Peter, it all went according to script."

A Closing Comment; The Transactional Lawyer's Prayer

Following the incident involving the agreement not to enforce the judgment and the attachment of the defendant's bank account, I asked one of my partners who was concerned by the attachment why he had not relied on my judgment. "I didn't know you could predict the future," came a subdued reply. What my partner did not appreciate was that when money and economic survival are on the line, the human animal, unless pushed too far, will act in a rational manner. And, in a given context, a person acting rationally is predictable.

Learning to negotiate effectively involves learning to read, understand and interpret—not what people say, not even people themselves, but situations. It is not unlike quarterbacks learning to read defenses or great running backs who grasp the entire flow of the defense and their offensive line and so know when to brake, cut and accelerate. But the key to this learning is not found in books or on casssette tapes or in classrooms. It comes only from experience. And the confidence to act on one's interpretation is bred from that experience coupled with the logic of the analysis. This confidence, then, must blend with imagination and flexibility to achieve the highest form of the art.

* * *

Most of the anecdotes displaying our acronym, "**BLIP**", have been—as unfortunately negotiations often are—confrontational in nature. True, there is an adversarial aspect to any negotiation. But, ideally, negotiations should not become confrontational, because the purpose and endgame of any negotiation is to solve problems—that is, **TO FIND SOLUTIONS**. So, to conclude, I'm going to tell you about the most satisfying, yet shortest and most boring negotiation of my entire career.

Again, that well-known, multinational company that I helped in the film deal, asked me to help resolve an impasse that their fancy international law firm had not been able to solve.

We met with the other party and its advisor, a young gentleman who was not a lawyer. I listened carefully as the parties explained their differences, and then asked to be excused with my client. I forget the details, but I asked whether the client would do a few things to accommodate the other party. "Yes, we can do that", came the reply. We returned to the meeting and I explained what our client was willing to do. The advisor to the other party then asked to be excused with his client. When they returned, he presented some modifications, all of which were fine with our client. Deal done!. No Combat! And that's why you pray for

> *THE PERSON ON THE OTHER SIDE OF THE TABLE TO BE THE SMARTEST PERSON IN THE WORLD.*

As you can see, in addition to being able to read situations well, good negotiators must also possess the qualities of skilled mediators.

And I do wish you all short, boring and successful negotiations.

* * *

Resource Materials: Negotiating

The following materials supplement the teaching in this Chapter. They are available on Westlaw to law students and their teachers without charge if the law school has a plan with Westlaw that includes *Commercial Agreements, infra.*

Commercial Agreements—A Lawyer's Guide to drafting and Negotiating, Thomson Reuters.

- Chapter 20: Rated "PG"
- Chapter 21: Rated "**R**"

Conclusion

Well, as Porky Pig would say,

Th … th … th … that's all for now folks.

Index

Q

R

S

T

U

V

W

X, Y, Z